due SOUTH™

THE OFFICIAL COMPANION

ALLIANCE®

due SOUTH

THE OFFICIAL COMPANION

Geoff Tibballs

TITAN BOOKS

DUE SOUTH
THE OFFICIAL COMPANION

ISBN 1 85286 928 3

Published by
Titan Books
42-44 Dolben Street
London SE1 0UP

First edition April 1998
10 9 8 7 6 5 4 3 2 1

Design by Caroline Grimshaw.
Production by Bob Kelly.

Due South photographs by Michael Courtney, Marni Grossman,
Michaelin McDermott, John Medland and Jeffery Newbury.

British Library Cataloguing-in-Publication Data.
A catalogue record for this book is available from the British Library.

ACKNOWLEDGEMENTS

Thank you kindly to Paul Gross, David Marciano, Callum Keith
Rennie, Jeff King, George Bloomfield, Rick Parker and Frank
Siracusa; to Robert Lantos, Christine Shipton, Rose Mangone,
Nancy Bassett and Carmite Sadeh at Alliance Communications;
to *Due South* publicist Nancy Manoogian; to Elaine Lucas; to
Anna Kingsley; and to Simon Furman, David Barraclough, Katy
Wild and Gillian Christie at Titan Books.

The author gratefully acknowledges the use of extra interview
material from the following publications: *Daily Star*, *Daily Mirror*,
E-TV, *Macleans*, *Ottawa Citizen*, *Radio Times*, *Toronto Star*, *TV
Guide*, *TV Times*, *TV Zone* and *Wall Street Journal*.

Check out the Official Due South web site at www.duesouth.com or for a
web site print out contact Custom Casuals, 67 Mowat Ave. Suite #134,
Toronto, ON, M6K 3E3, Canada. Tel: (416) 533 3135

Detective Armani can be contacted via Elaine Lucas at 43 Old Hall Drive,
Bamber Bridge, Preston PR5 6EX.

Printed and bound in Great Britain by Stephens and George Ltd, Merthyr
Industrial Estate, Dowlais, Merthyr Tydfil.

CONTENTS

6 INTRODUCTION

8 *season* **ONE**
10 THE BIRTH OF DUE SOUTH
14 SEASON HIGHLIGHTS: THE PILOT
18 ROLL CALL: FRASER, VECCHIO, FRASER SR,
'BUCK' FROBISHER
26 CREATING DUE SOUTH
34 SEASON HIGHLIGHTS: MANHUNT
36 LET'S HEAR IT FOR DIEFENBAKER
38 SEASON HIGHLIGHTS: THE WILD BUNCH
40 ROLL CALL: LT WELSH, HUEY, LOUIS, ELAINE
44 SEASON HIGHLIGHTS: VICTORIA'S SECRET

50 *season* **TWO**
52 DEAF EARS, LOUD VOICES (SEASON OVERVIEW)
54 SEASON HIGHLIGHTS: BIRD IN THE HAND
56 LINES OF LATITUDE (CLASSIC DIALOGUE)
58 SEASON HIGHLIGHTS: JULIET IS BLEEDING
62 POLITE OFFICER — PAUL GROSS SPEAKS
66 RAY OF HOPE — DAVID MARCIANO SPEAKS
68 SEASON HIGHLIGHTS: SOME LIKE IT RED
70 ROLL CALL: THATCHER, VICTORIA, FRANCESCA
74 SEASON HIGHLIGHTS: ALL THE QUEEN'S HORSES

78 *season* **THREE**
80 GLAD TIDINGS (SEASON OVERVIEW)
82 SEASON HIGHLIGHTS: BURNING DOWN THE HOUSE
86 ROLL CALL: KOWALSKI
88 HEADS YOU WIN — CALLUM KEITH RENNIE SPEAKS

90 EPISODE GUIDE

goin' DUE SOUTH

A COP, A MOUNTIE AND A PLEASANTLY SKEWED SENSE OF HUMOUR

Above: Fraser with his new sidekick Stanley Kowalski (Callum Keith Rennie).

TAKE ONE SQUARE-JAWED, ramrod-straight Mountie from Canada's snow covered north, plant him in the heart of Chicago (a contradiction in terms to most Canadians), add a streetwise American cop and a deaf, lip-reading wolf, and you have the recipe for one of the most innovative and offbeat television shows in recent years.

But *Due South* is more than just another good buddy cop show. Its quirky storylines, witty dialogue and evident delight in sending up both Canadians and Americans in equal measure give it a uniqueness and a charm all of its own.

Constable Benton Fraser of the Royal Canadian Mounted Police arrives in Chicago as a fish out of water in search of the killer of his equally fine, upstanding Mountie father. Between duties at the city's Canadian Consulate (where he often stands as doorman), he enlists the services of the reluctant Detective Ray Vecchio of the Chicago Police Department. Together they not only crack that case but combat all manner of crime, frequently with the help of Fraser's pet wolf Diefenbaker, a sort of Lassie with menaces.

In the process, *Due South* mocks the Canadian and American national stereotypes with a subtlety and irony which has sometimes been lost on audiences.

Canadians are seen by Americans as immaculately groomed and terminally polite, and so Fraser is courteous at all times (his trademark "Thank you kindly" quickly emerged as the show's catchphrase), even when he is facing extreme adversity. He gives generously to street beggars and would rather appeal to a criminal's better nature than use force. Since Fraser isn't licensed to use a gun in the United States, he ventures on to the mean streets of Chicago unarmed. Ray finds such behaviour incomprehensible in a city where, for safety, even the muggers go around in pairs.

By contrast, the vast majority of Canadians see Americans as gun-toting, fast-talking and loud-dressing. Ray Vecchio more than lives up to all three stereotypes. Whereas Fraser likes to employ human psychology and Inuit wisdom to gain the better of his opponent, Ray favours the more direct approach. "Being an American, I know where my strength lies," he says, emptying two revolvers, an automatic, two extra clips, three speed loaders and a switch blade from his pocket. "And that is in being as heavily armed as possible at all times."

Invariably, it is Fraser's unorthodox methods, coupled with his uncanny tracking skills — which often involve putting a wide variety of unsavoury substances to his mouth — that pay dividends.

With the advent of season three, and a new sidekick for Fraser in the shape of young, brash and volatile cop Stanley Kowalski, an equally offbeat and unlikely partnership has evolved, taking the series into exciting and previously uncharted territory. It may seem unwise to tamper with such winning chemistry, but then *Due South* has always been the sort of show to confound expectations.

With so many cop shows around, why has *Due South* built up such a devoted following? Could it be the surreal situations and mantle of superhero which give Fraser and his partner the air of a latter-day Batman and Robin? Is it the combination of off-beat humour with genuine moments of high drama in a gritty urban setting? Or is it that Fraser's clean-cut courtesy is a welcome throwback to the days when people didn't only speak to others in city streets to relieve them of their valuables? Or, as Paul Gross's legion of female fans insist, does he simply look good in a uniform?

Whatever the answer, let's just be grateful for it. ▼

"Thank you kindly."

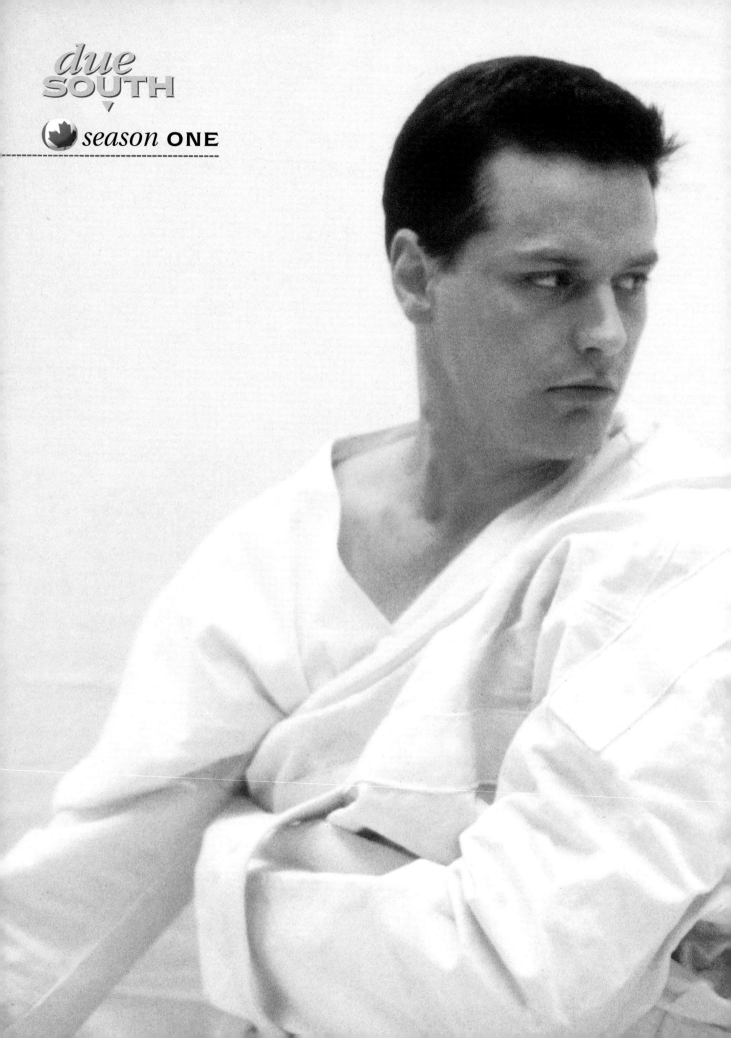

due
SOUTH

season ONE

STRAIGHT
jackets

NEW DIRECTION
The birth of DUE SOUTH

THANKS, BUT NO THANKS.
THE PRE-SEASON ONE SEARCH FOR STARS

IT WAS ROBERT LANTOS, THE Chairman and CEO of Alliance Communications in Toronto, who first came up with the idea for a series about a Canadian trapper or a Mountie; someone who moves from way up in the frozen north to big city USA. Lantos and the then president of CBS, Jeff Sagansky, who wanted "something different they could shoot in Canada," further developed the project. Sagansky approached Canadian writer Paul Haggis, acclaimed for his work on, among others, *thirtysomething* (for which he won an Emmy), *LA Law* and *The Tracey Ullman Show*, and it was he who finally gave the show its title: *Due South*.

To say Haggis was underwhelmed by the project is putting it mildly. "I thought it was the worst idea I'd ever heard!" he remembers. "I sat around feeling sorry for myself, thinking: 'Why do the networks always do this to me?' But the more I thought about it, the more I saw the comic potential in such a situation and I began to realise that I could twist it around a bit and have a lot of fun with the characters."

For his inspiration, Haggis turned to such classic American television series as *Sergeant Preston of the Yukon*.

"I created Fraser, based on all those great serials from the 1950s," admits Haggis, "and then, having created the perfect, stereotypical Canadian, I said: 'OK, that's what Americans think of

> *"First dirt tasting, now piddle-sniffing. I don't want to be around when you start listening to dung."*

Above: In 'Free Willie', Fraser and Vecchio take the reins of a horse-drawn carriage in pursuit of villains.

Canadians. So, what do Canadians think about Americans?'

"'Well,' I said to myself, 'they think they all pack guns, they are incredibly rude, shoot first, ask questions later.' So I came up with Ray. When I had the two of them, I had a show."

It was to prove much harder, however, to cast the two leads, as Haggis recalls: "We searched for about six months to find our Mountie. We cast in Toronto, Vancouver, Los Angeles, New York and London. Early on, the casting director said, 'You have to see this guy Paul Gross.' I said, 'Who the hell is he?' and they sent me a tape of a drama Paul had done where he plays a character during the war of 1812 or something like that. He was dressed as a redcoat and sitting astride a horse. He looked ridiculous!"

The search for an actor who could skilfully combine the various elements of Fraser's character continued without success for the next few months, and on several occasions Paul Gross's name resurfaced as a potential candidate.

"Finally I said, 'OK, I'll meet with this guy.' He walked in and within two minutes, I knew he was Fraser," says Haggis. "He had such a wicked sense of humour. I was so glad that he accepted the part. Paul was the only person I found who could do the role and walk that fine line between drama and comedy. He played it with just enough tongue-in-cheek and was able to say some of those incredibly corny lines and still make them sound sincere."

For his part, Paul Gross had reser-

Above: Goin'...? Neither Paul Gross nor David Marciano were initially sure that *Due South* was the right direction for their careers.

vations: "At the time I just wasn't interested in doing a series. I didn't want to get locked into something for a long period of time. I was living in Malibu, California, and reading scripts that were all pretty appalling. They approached me with an offer [to do *Due South*] and I didn't even read the script. I just said, 'No thanks.'

"Some months later they came back

> ## "I was resentful, naturally. So the next day I took the present and attempted to feed it to a passing walrus."

and asked me if I would at least read it," continues Gross. "It still sounded pretty goofy but I did, and thought it was one of the funniest things I'd ever read. The only sensible course of action was to do it. But I never thought it would last more than four episodes because the show was so oddball."

The search for Ray was equally time-consuming. "When David Marciano finally came in to read," recalls Paul Haggis, "the first thing he said was, 'I can't play this guy'. But the way he said it, I knew he was Ray."

A year later, Marciano was still not on board. Despite Haggis's best efforts to convince him that he was perfect for the role, something about the character refused to gel.

Marciano remembers: "When I first received the material for the *Due South* movie, I worked on it with my wife, actress Katayoun Amini, but I just could

Top: No job too small. "I'm strictly misdemeanours," purse snatcher Willie Lambert laments in 'Free Willie'.
Above: Ray — heavily armed as always.

not get it. The script was good and the writing solid, but I had trouble understanding the character of Ray Vecchio. When I read a part, I play with it and try to make it sing. With me, it's not an intellectual process of crafting, it's more of an artistic thing of just feeling it. For some reason I just couldn't get the rhythm of the character, so I passed on the audition."

But while Marciano seemed unable to see himself as Ray, pressure from those who clearly did mounted. Marciano once more found himself at odds with the character:

"My agent called me and said: 'They really want to see you. They think you're perfect for the part.' I worked on it again with my wife, but still wasn't happy. My agent pleaded with me to go in, so I did. I read the first three lines and they came out really stilted. I stopped and said: 'I apologise. I think

Above: Do you come here often? Fraser meets a very different type of 'Mountie' in 'Chicago Holiday', but still manages to maintain his cool. Somehow we doubt that this uniform is RCMP approved.

RCMP

RENOWNED FOR ALWAYS GETTING THEIR man (although their motto is in fact 'Maintiens le droit' — 'Uphold the right'), the Royal Canadian Mounted Police enforce the law in all Canadian provinces except Quebec and Ontario, who have their own provincial police. But even there, Mounties are often called in to assist the local forces.

Founded in 1873 as the North West Mounted Police, they changed their name in 1920, by which time they had earned respect for bringing a degree of law and order to the violent North West Territories.

Today's Mounties are spread over more than 700 posts and the service also boasts naval and air divisions, plus crime-detection laboratories. Although there is a regulation brown uniform, as worn by Fraser when performing routine police duties, the Mounties' most familiar attire is their parade uniform of a low, broad-brimmed hat, scarlet jacket and blue trousers with a yellow stripe. The force always takes great pride in its appearance, its military bearing, its ceremonial horse shows and — of course — its ability to sing heartily at all times.

the whole project is great, the script is wonderful and the character is really interesting, but this isn't for me.'

"When I got home, I got another call from my agent, saying they wanted me back again, this time to work with the director. Paul Gross was also going to be there so I went and did it. They said: 'Great. Listen, when you go to read in front of the network executives you need to be a little shorter than Paul, so wear really flat shoes', because Paul and I are roughly the same height. I went in to the network audition and after each reading things just got worse and worse. I began to care less, but at the same time I cared more. I was becoming more and more confused, yet somehow I landed the part."

With the leading actors in place, all that remained was to perfect their on-screen chemistry. ▼

THE *pilot*

WRITTEN BY SERIES CREATOR PAUL Haggis, the Pilot storyline was inspired by the James Bay Power Project, which left over 10,000 caribou mysteriously drowned in the forests of Northern Canada when the 'rivers ran backwards' (the Canadian government maintains they died as a result of a series of freak natural occurrences). The episode superbly interweaves the serious environmental message and the business of Fraser tracking down his father's killer with a host of memorable comic scenes.

An early example of *Due South*'s unique sense of humour comes when Fraser (a name change from the original Sturges), sensing skulduggery afoot, dumps a dead caribou onto the slab at the local morgue, to be greeted by the coroner's deadpan response: "Pet, was it?" Later on, the first person Fraser encounters in Chicago is a missionary urging, "Help feed the hungry." Ever eager to help, Fraser slips a bar of pemmican into the begging bowl with the advice: "If you're still hungry when you

finish it, drink water. It expands in your stomach." Still at the airport, he foolishly loans $100 to a beggar claiming

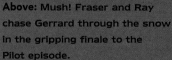

Above: Mush! Fraser and Ray chase Gerrard through the snow in the gripping finale to the Pilot episode.

to need the cash for his little girl's operation. It seems he has a lot to learn about city life.

Greeted by the desk sergeant as Nanook of the North, Fraser proceeds to blow Ray's cover at the first attempt by going to the holding cell and asking for Detective Armani (Ray was posing as a felon in a bid to bust a series of fashion heists). But Fraser soon earns Ray's grudging respect for his ingenious powers of detection. Ray himself is hardly orthodox — he recognises Drake, the hitman hired to kill Fraser Sr., by his nose. "I never forget a nose," he says. The search for Drake takes the pair to a run-down joint where the only thing that's neat is the bourbon. With every customer armed to the teeth, Fraser politely requests all illegal weapons to be placed on the bar, his naïveté compounded when he helpfully informs the assembled throng that, because he has no local licence, his own gun is empty. Amazingly, they cooperate, but all hell then breaks loose as Drake makes

his escape by firing indiscriminately into the crowd.

Drake is eventually gunned down by the man who hired him, Fraser Sr.'s old Mountie colleague Gerrard, and the climax takes Fraser and Ray to the frozen north for a chase through the snow in pursuit of their prey. Typically, Ray dresses for a weekend in Aspen.

Finally, Fraser and Gerrard come face-to-face, but Fraser resists the temptation to exact full revenge for his father's murder.

With Gerrard safely under lock and key, Fraser receives a visit from the airport beggar who pays him back his $100. Fraser's faith in human nature remains intact.

The wilderness scenes were shot in the Yukon. Paul Haggis says: "I still have fond memories of standing on a mountain top, directing the dog-sled/snowmobile chase, while talking to CBS on my cell phone!"

But filming was dogged by misfortune, as Paul Gross remembers: "For one scene we needed to have a dead caribou. Since white civilians are not allowed to go in and hunt caribou without various permits, we hired Eskimo hunters to do it for us, but we neglected to bury the carcass with the appropriate ritual. An Eskimo gentleman named Eric, who was on the show, had phoned up the production office and said, 'You have to make sure you tend to the caribou corpse. If not, you'll end up with a curse on this project.'

"It all has to do with their legends," continues Gross, "and sure enough things started to go wrong.

"WHAT DO THEY SHOOT PEOPLE WITH IN CANADA? SERVIETTES?"

We were using this little plane in the background of a scene. When the pilot took off, the plane cartwheeled, hit a building, slammed into one of our trucks and crumpled. We had car accidents, snowmobile problems and all this other weird stuff going on, and it followed us back to Toronto where we accidentally blew up a strategic location. A guy was supposed to shoot a gun and blow up a mirror, but they put in too many explosive charges and we blew up this famous bar called the El Macambo. There we were standing around at three o'clock in the morning with no place to film. We finally had to acknowledge the curse as real and took the caribou to a shaman on the Six Nations Reserve for a proper burial ceremony. After that, our luck began to improve!"

The response to the Pilot movie exceeded all expectations. Jeff King, who had joined as producer mid-way through, remembers: "It broke all kinds of records in Canada. I think it was something like the most-watched two-hour movie of the season. We certainly didn't expect it to be such a huge success."

Paul Gross echoes his sentiments. "the Pilot

was very challenging and the comedy proved to be difficult. Looking back at it, I think we probably got close to sixty per cent of it right. We missed a lot of stuff. I think most of us just couldn't see how the hell anyone else would watch it. This was particularly true in the case of American television, which seems to exist on such a narrow

Top: Fraser appeals for calm in a Chicago bar. Fat chance.
Above: The reckoning. Fraser catches up with his father's killer.

Above: One man and his wolf — Fraser and Diefenbaker, played (for the one and only time) by malamute Frankie.

bandwidth, and because the Pilot fell between the two stools of action and comedy, it just didn't seem to be very promising. So I think everyone was surprised when it continued as a series."

CBS wasted no time, quickly commissioning thirteen episodes. Changes were minimal. Captain Walsh from the Pilot became Lt Welsh in the series and Beau Starr, who had been unavailable, took over the role. Three brand new supporting characters — Detectives Huey and (Louis) Gardino

and Civilian Aide Elaine Besbriss — were added to the police station personnel, and malamute Frankie was replaced by Siberian husky Lincoln as Diefenbaker.

The first episode, 'Free Willie', quickly established one of the other main locations — Fraser's slum apartment building. The opening scene sees Ray driving Fraser to his new accommodation, all the while trying to convince him that no sane person would want to live in such a run-down and crime-ridden area. Fraser is pragmatic: "It's central, convenient, I can walk to work in seven minutes." "Not without backup," warns Ray, but to no avail. Despite such features as "the decorative graffiti motif" and "the clever use of plumbing to create the waterfall effect", Fraser and Diefenbaker are soon in residence. Ray, ultimately, is philosophical, telling Diefenbaker not to worry... "You'll have plenty to hunt in here."

All *Due South*'s key characters (bar Inspector Thatcher) and locations were in place, and any fine details (such as slight changes to Fraser's uniform to bring it into line with official RCMP dress code) were likewise swiftly resolved.

NORTH WEST TERRITORIES

IN A COUNTRY NOTED FOR ITS HOSPITALITY, there is little that is hospitable about the North West Territories. Winter temperatures in this part of Canada can drop to minus fifty degrees centigrade, so anything approaching freezing point has the locals reaching for the Ambre Solaire. Straddling the Arctic Circle, the Territories cover 3,426,320 sq km (1,322,904 sq miles) — one-third of the total of Canada — and have thousands of islands in addition to the main land mass. Not surprisingly, the sea is covered in ice for much of the year.

Fraser was raised in Inuvik and Tuktoyaktuk, two settlements in the far north west near to where the Mackenzie River flows into the Beaufort Sea. With a population of just one person for every fifty-nine sq km, you are more likely to run into caribou, moose, wolves or bears. Fur-trapping, once the most important industry, is in decline although it is still carried on by some Native Americans. Instead, minerals are now the major economic resource as the barren landscape is mined for its deposits of gold, silver, uranium, zinc, iron ore, tungsten and lead.

"JUST TELL HIM TO STAY... AND NOT TO EAT ANYTHING WITH AN EMBLEM ON IT."

CONSTABLE BENTON FRASER

RAISED IN A DISTANT OUTPOST OF THE North West Territories by his librarian grandparents (his mother having died when he was just six), young Benton Fraser idolised his Mountie father, Robert, and eventually followed him into the RCMP.

He soon began to display the same zeal as his father for upholding the law, once tracking a man 3,000 kilometres through one of the worst snowstorms in memory just for fishing over the limit. Fraser was regularly sent to distant outposts (if only to stop him irritating his fellow officers), where he learned a great deal from the Inuit. Even today, if anyone has a few hours (or maybe a day) to spare, Fraser will regale them with an Inuit tale.

An urban existence held little interest for Fraser. A posting to Moose Jaw ended after just five weeks because he was unable to adjust to big city life. Not surprisingly, he arrived in Chicago with only the barest essentials — a backpack containing his bedroll, camping gear and, most important of all, his uniforms.

His spartan apartment is scarcely a typical bachelor pad. He borrows most domestic appliances — such as vacuums — from his crafty city neighbours, who lend him the items

on condition that he has them repaired before they are returned. Naturally enough, Fraser is only too happy to oblige.

For the most part, Fraser's tidy and ordered mind is uncluttered by thoughts of romance. Women find him attractive, but he feels uncomfortable about such matters. The sole exception is bank robber Victoria Metcalf, whom Fraser is convinced is the only woman he will ever love.

Mountie uniforms have played a significant role in the life of Paul Gross. The last time he wore one prior to

Above: Fraser in 'Chicago Holiday', oblivious as ever to the fact that women find him irresistible.

Due South was in a 1985 play in Ottawa, in which a young actress named Martha Burns played an Indian squaw. It was love at first sight and three years later the pair married. They now live in Toronto with their two children — Hannah, aged seven, and Jack, aged four.

Paul Gross was born in Calgary, Alberta, in April 1960, the son of an army tank commander. After living on an army base in Alberta for the first five years of his life, Paul came to England for two years when his father was posted to Surrey. He remembers: "On an army base, your main entertainment was to go around punching other kids. I carried on the same way at school in Surrey, so I was sent home on a weekly basis for beating up the others. But by the time I left I had an English accent. I'd become civilised!"

Following further education in Germany and Washington DC, Gross returned to Canada where he fell into acting almost by default. Having gained his drama degree, he then performed extensively in Canadian regional theatres and began to forge a writing career. His first play, *The Deer and the Antelope Play*, picked up two awards, and a terrorism-based episode

"I MEAN, IF I WANT ANYBODY TO SLEEP WITH MY SISTER — AND I'M NOT ENCOURAGING THIS — I'D WANT IT TO BE YOU."

FRASER'S HAT

WHEREAS MOST COPS IN CHICAGO would welcome the security of a bullet-proof vest, Fraser feels safe enough provided he is wearing his Mountie stetson. He sees it as a symbol of the law, one that will offer him protection at all times.

Certainly whenever he is without it, something awful seems to happen. In 'Victoria's Secret', his hat is lost on the street and Diefenbaker ends up getting shot. At the end of the same episode, a hatless Fraser is himself shot. In 'Manhunt', the hat flies off his head and he's stabbed in the leg. After he and his headgear have parted company in 'The Deal', Fraser is beaten up; in 'Mask', he loses his hat on the museum roof and sub-sequently falls off; while in 'Flash-back', the loss of his hat as he is thrown from the van coincides with the onset of amnesia.

Given the hat's significance, it should come as no surprise that Fraser should offer it to Ray as protection from the cold when the pair are sealed in a frozen meat locker in 'They Eat Horses, Don't They?'. For Fraser, the gift of his hat is the ultimate act of friendship.

Above: In 'An Invitation to Romance', Fraser sweeps yet another woman off her feet.

of *For the Record* later earned him a Best TV Drama nomination at the 1986 Gemini Awards. He received another Gemini nomination for Best Writer for the *Due South* episode 'All The Queen's Horses'. As an actor, his roles have included a ski instructor in the movie *Aspen Extreme*, a waiter with an eye for the women in *Tales of the City*, and a recent appearance in a remake of *20,000 Leagues Under the Sea*. Gross has won two Best Actor Geminis (1995 and 1996) for his portrayal of Constable Benton Fraser. ▼

Above: Fraser minus hat inevitably equals disaster (see left). A tense scene from 'Letting Go'.

DETECTIVE RAY VECCHIO

RAY VECCHIO HAS ALWAYS FOUND IT difficult to live up to the title of plainclothes detective. There's nothing wrong with his detective work, but his clothes — garish shirts and Armani suits — are far from plain. Ray's excuse is that they're to blend in with the criminal fraternity, but it's no small wonder he hasn't been arrested for wearing a loud shirt in a built-up area. If nothing else, Ray's designer attire certainly reflects his larger than life personality.

Part of a large, excitable, close-knit Italian-American family, Ray shares the house left to him by his father with his mother, his divorced sister Francesca, and his married sister Maria and her good-for-nothing husband Tony. His situation is the total opposite of Fraser's spartan 'one man and his wolf' lifestyle.

A born cynic, Ray thought he'd done it all and seen it all until he met Fraser. At first his wisecracks seemed wasted on the po-faced Canadian, and Ray was irked by Fraser's peculiar investigation techniques. But when he realised they shared a common goal of bringing criminals to justice, they became best buddies. Ray even started to appreciate his new

partner's style... up to a point. Ray drew the line at sniffing things on the pavement.

If there's a true passion in Ray's life, it comes on four wheels. His pride and joy is his green 1971 Buick Riviera, and

Above: David Marciano as Ray Vecchio in 'You Must Remember This' — unlucky in love, cars and just about everything else.

when he was forced to blow it up to save his and Fraser's lives (in the season one episode 'The Man Who Knew Too Little') he immediately found himself another identical model, only for the second 'Riv' to be destroyed by the car bomb which killed Detective Gardino. So now he's on number three. Just as well then he doesn't get to see what happens to his beloved car in the season three opener 'Burning Down the House'.

It's much the same story with women. Since his divorce from Angie, the only woman to pluck his heart strings, apart from a brief fling with State's Attorney Louise St Laurent, was ATF agent Suzanne Chapin who ran him over, shot at him and then bludgeoned him about the head with her gun. Perhaps she was trying to tell him something.

David Marciano was born in Newark, New Jersey, in 1960 and, by his own admission, was a rebellious youth: "I was hanging around on street corners, drinking, gambling, playing cards, going to the racetrack, shooting pool, all those kind of things." At seventeen, Marciano was involved in a near fatal car crash. "I'd been partying all weekend," David says,

"IT'S A SICK COUNTRY YOU HAVE, FRASER."

"and I fell asleep while driving home. The next thing I knew the car hit one road barrier, then another, and almost got hit by oncoming traffic. I was very lucky to survive."

David enrolled at Northeastern University, Boston, where he studied biomedical engineering. After one "less than stellar year", he tried economics and accounting, but hated both. "One day," David recalls, "I called my mom complaining about school and she reminded me of an aptitude test I had taken back in high school which suggested my abilities lay in three areas — mathematics, architecture and acting. I chose acting..."

After working as a bartender between theatre jobs in Boston, David moved to Los Angeles in 1985 and got his first break as guest star in an episode of the cop series *Wiseguy*. David went on to play poet and bike messenger Jeffrey in *Civil Wars* and appear in *Duet*, *China Beach*, *Lethal Weapon II* and *Gypsy*. Settled at last, he is happily married to Katayoun Amini (who played Ray's ex-wife Angie), with whom he has a two-year-old daughter, Ariana Grace. ▼

"ARE YOU TELLING THAT STORY FOR MY BENEFIT? BECAUSE A) I DON'T BELIEVE IT AND B) I DON'T CARE."

CHICAGO

THE THIRD LARGEST CITY IN THE UNITED States, Chicago is situated on the south west shore of Lake Michigan at the mouth of the Chicago River. Home to the world's first skyscraper and some of the world's tallest buildings (including the 1,454 ft high Sears Tower), Chicago is known as the Windy City, partly on account of the breezes from Lake Michigan but also because its politicians are said to talk loud and long.

A major port and industrial centre, Chicago's most notorious era was during the years of Prohibition from 1920-33, when the city was run by gangsters such as Al 'Scarface' Capone, George 'Bugsy' Moran and others with silly nicknames.

Above: Down in the dumps. If there is one person destined to end up in the garbage, it's Ray.

Above: Ray and Dief.
Left: In 'Pizzas and Promises' Fraser goes undercover... as Ray?!

SERGEANT ROBERT FRASER

EVERYONE THOUGHT THAT SGT Robert Fraser was a one-off. Then along came his son Benton, a chip off the same ice block. To have one member of the family join the Mounties was bad luck; to have two was the force's worst nightmare. Not that there was anything wrong with old Bob Fraser. On the contrary, he was a dedicated law enforcer, with a record as unblemished as the Canadian snow. Indeed, he was killed because he wouldn't turn a blind eye to his fellow Mountie Gerrard's dishonesty. It was just that Bob set such impossible standards — he once booked his own wife for a traffic violation.

Now that he's dead, Fraser Sr. appears as a ghost to offer his son pearls of wisdom in times of crisis... whether he really wants them or not.

Sixty-five-year-old Newfound-land-born actor/writer Gordon Pinsent, who plays Bob Fraser, was brought back from the dead

Left: It takes a certain kind of man to book his own wife for a traffic violation. Bob Fraser was that man.

thanks to series co-creator Paul Haggis. "I had so much fun working on the Pilot with Gordon," explains Paul. "We were sitting around a Yukon bar one night after work and I told him, 'I'm going to bring you back.' He said to me, 'But you just killed me.' So I wrote 'The Gift of the Wheelman' where the ghost of Fraser Sr. comes back. We created an epic hero in him and I figured it must be very difficult for Benton to live under his shadow. I thought if I kept him around all the time, he'd become incredibly annoying."

Married to actress Charmion King (their daughter Leah has also taken to the stage), Pinsent is the creator of such well-known works as *The Rowdyman*, *John and the Missus* and *A Gift to Last*. Pinsent has worn the scarlet jacket no less than three times in career: as Sgt Scott in the sixties children's series *The Forest Rangers*, as Sgt Edgar Sturgess in *A Gift to Last*, and now in *Due South*. ▼

Right: As a youngster, Fraser always wanted to spend more time with his father. Sometimes it pays to be careful what you wish for.

"WELL, THERE WAS YOUR UNCLE TIBERIUS, WHO DIED WRAPPED IN CABBAGE LEAVES, BUT WE ASSUMED THAT WAS A FREAK ACCIDENT."

SERGEANT DUNCAN 'BUCK' FROBISHER

SGT DUNCAN 'BUCK' FROBISHER IS AN old Mountie friend of Bob Fraser. In their prime, the pair were feared by the Canadian criminal fraternity for their ruthless determination to bring their man back at all costs. Expert shots, they fought for the love of the same woman, they shared jokes, stories and the same high moral ground.

In fact the only thing they don't have in common is that Buck is still breathing. Leafing through his father's diary, young Benton Fraser read epic tales of Buck's heroism — the stuff of which legends are made — but Buck then fell on hard times, becoming a shadow of his former glory, until Fraser gave him back his self-respect in 'Manhunt'.

Born in Regina, Saskatchewan, in 1925, Leslie Nielsen made his name as a radio disc jockey and appeared in serious cop shows such as *The New Breed* and *The Protectors*, before

This page: Frobisher was the name of the sixteenth century explorer who discovered Baffin Island in search of the North West Passage.

displaying a superb flair for deadpan comedy in the 1980 film spoof *Airplane!*. Two years later, he kept a straight face as Detective Frank Drebin in the hilarious TV series *Police Squad*, reprising the role in the subsequent *Naked Gun* movie spin-offs. Other recent credits include *Spy Hard*, *Rent-a-Kid* and *Dracula: Dead and Loving It*. He also does a nice line in 'Bad Golf' videos. On and off-set, he is a renowned practical joker with a disturbing penchant for whoopee cushions, something which Paul Gross soon caught wind of. "He's a master at it!" exclaims Gross with due appreciation. "He gave me one of those things and said: 'I've got to pass this on to you. I'm getting old, and someone has to take this up!'" ▼

"ALRIGHT. PRIORITIES. ONE: DEFUSE THE TRAIN. TWO: STOP THE BOMB."

due NORTH

CHICAGO COMES TO TORONTO

Left: The blazing car sequence in the season three opener 'Burning Down the House'.
Opposite: Easy Rider. Paul Gross poses atop the train in 'All The Queen's Horses'.

ALTHOUGH *DUE SOUTH* IS set in Chicago, virtually all of the filming is done in and around Toronto. Apart from a few establishing shots of Chicago — such as Ray's Buick Riviera driving along the streets — all of the city life you see on screen is Toronto. But the transformation has not been easy, for Chicago and Toronto are like chalk and cheese. Peter Ustinov once called Toronto "New York as if run by the Swiss", and the city prides itself on its tidiness, in stark contrast to Chicago's gritty urban mix of litter and graffiti.

To compensate for Toronto's lack of decay, the art department on *Due South* have to dump garbage and spray mock graffiti in the areas in which they are filming. Knowing little about such a non-Canadian phenomenon as urban graffiti, the designers initially went about this task with a textbook in one hand and a can of spray paint in the other. Shooting one of the early episodes required the creation of a litter-strewn alley. The art department went about their business, 'dirtied

up' the alley and, after a successful morning's filming, everybody broke for lunch. It was then that a resident phoned the City of Toronto maintenance department to complain about

> *"Brand new paint job, waxed and detailed. You have any idea what windows for a Buick Riviera go for?!"*

the state of the alley. Engineers arrived on the scene within minutes and, seeing no sign of activity, promptly hauled away all the carefully-arranged garbage. "We had to fight to get it back," laughs Jeff King. "Those sanitation engineers were tough. They pride themselves on a clean street."

Other less drastic alterations also have to be made to complete the metamorphosis of Chicago into Toronto. All of the vehicle licence plates have to be changed, along with street signs, bus shelters, fire hydrants, telephone boxes and post boxes (in Canada they are red; in the United States they are grey/blue). To get around the expense of constant location filming, studio sets were built for the station interior, Fraser's apartment and the Consulate interior. Some of these sets were destroyed at the end of the second season and the Consulate is now filmed in a vacant mansion on the university campus in downtown Toronto. Each episode takes an average of eight days to shoot, but before that there are two intensive weeks of pre-production

Above: Filming 'The Promise'. Graffiti courtesy of the art department.

Above: George Bloomfield directs Gordon Pinsent and Paul Gross in 'Burning Down the House'.

and then afterwards a further few weeks of post-production — which includes editing, dubbing and the adding on of incidental music.

One of the most familiar sights on *Due South* has been Ray's car. In total, there have been seven duplicate green 1971 Buick Rivieras (green was chosen because it was the easiest colour to find), mostly tracked down via the small ads in papers. The reason so many have been needed is that they have been wrecked by the various collisions and explosions which have beset Ray's treasured automobile.

Indeed, the spectacular

Above: The stunt doubles take over in 'Burning Down the House'.

stunts are an integral part of *Due South* and whereas some actors need a stunt double just to tie their shoelaces (actually it was Leslie Nielsen who taught Paul Gross how to lace the special Mountie boots), Gross prefers to do the majority of Fraser's stunts himself. "It always looks better on screen if you do your own stunts," he says, "and it's also faster. If you use a stunt man, it takes three or four scenes, cutting to and fro, and it takes time to set all these things up. The only occasions when I don't do my own stunts is if I get a feeling that something's too dangerous or if

Above: Filming on the streets of Chicago... er, Toronto.

it's unnecessary for me to do it, say for example if the scene isn't a close-up of Fraser. If it's just a long shot, there's really no point me doing it.

"Occasionally there's a stunt I want to do, but I'm not allowed to. In the season three opener, 'Fraser is seen jumping into a boat from an eighty foot cliff. I was keen to do that jump but in fact the pool of water we used was so shallow that they wouldn't even let the stunt man do it. So in the end I jumped off a sixty foot cliff into an airbag and that was cut into a long shot of the stunt man. It was great fun, but unfortunately we did it in one take. I wanted to do it all over again!"

The same episode sees the blazing car being driven through the streets — a scene which caused a few raised

"They said he was agile! He's not agile. He fell off the car!"

eyebrows among passers-by — before plunging into the water (Toronto Harbour doubled for Lake Michigan). For the first stage of this dramatic sequence, Paul Gross had to be filmed on top of a car travelling at around 30mph. "That was pretty hairy because there wasn't much protection. Some of those scenes were done with a camera car on a platform, so if I'd fallen off I'd have landed on the platform. That wouldn't have been too bad, but for other scenes there was no platform and if I'd fallen off then, it could have been

nasty. When the fire broke out, it was extraordinarily hot in that car. Callum Keith Rennie (who plays Fraser's new partner, Kowalski) and I could only do two or three takes at a time before we had to get out."

As the fire intensified, stunt men, their bodies covered in fire-retardant gel, replaced the actors inside the car and for the final sequence dummies were strapped into the vehicle to represent Fraser and Kowalski. The car was hooked to an out-of-shot cable and pulled into the water.

Since Paul Gross wrote the script for that episode, he has nobody to blame but himself. "Whenever I'm doing a script, I'm always conscious about including plenty of exciting stunts because that's part of the show's appeal."

That was the case in 'All The Queen's Horses' where Fraser and Inspector Meg Thatcher (Camilla Scott) found themselves on top of a moving train rumbling through the Canadian countryside at 40mph. Much to director George Bloomfield's consternation, Gross and Scott insisted on doing the scene where their characters ran along the top of the moving train in person. "I hate that stuff," admits Bloomfield, "but they convinced me it was safe." Neither actor wore a harness — in fact the only person who did was the steadicam operator filming the sequence. However, Gross's stunt double, Ken Quinn, did take over for the scene where Fraser fell off the train.

Above and below: Paul Gross takes an active behind-the-scenes role, here on the set of 'All The Queen's Horses'.

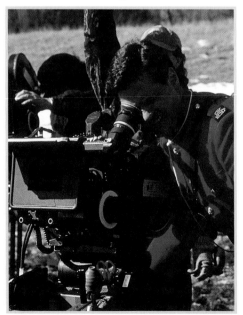

Above and top: Paul Gross and Callum Keith Rennie had to spend three days in a water tank to film underwater scenes for 'Mountie on the Bounty'.

storeys up. There were no safety nets but I wore a harness with a cable running up my arm. I knew that cable could hold up a car, so I felt in safe hands. I'm not afraid of heights, but although intellectually you say it's safe, when you look over the edge, your body says, 'Get back up!' And to be honest, when you're up there, you don't have time to be afraid — you're too busy concentrating on acting the scene. In the end I just thought, Fraser knows how to jump so I'll be okay!"

George Bloomfield has directed some of the key episodes of *Due South*. One of his most complicated shoots was the ice-skating chase in 'The Blue Line' for which two blocks of Toronto streets were closed to traffic and iced over. "It took about three nights," says Bloomfield. "The problem was that after icing the streets over, the weather got warmer and we were rushing to film on this rapidly melting set. And it was freezing cold the day we shot the egg fight in 'We Are the Eggmen'. Everybody was worried about the chickens getting cold — not about the actors and director, just the chickens!"

But as far as Paul Gross is concerned, for sheer discomfort nothing can compare to the season three finale, 'Mountie on the Bounty', where Fraser

"You shouldn't have pressed the hot wax option."

Above: Paul Gross discusses a scene with Steve DiMarco (director).

"It all seemed fairly safe to me," says Gross. "We've got a great crew and I have tremendous faith in them. We've only ever had one injury in the history of the show and that was when a stunt man fell off a building in the very first episode, 'Free Willie'. Funnily enough, it's doing the easier things where you tend to get hurt. Big stunts are usually very safe because so much preparation goes into them, so I reckon I'm safer hanging over the side of a building than running around alleys. It's when you least expect it that you have problems.

"In the new series, Fraser had to hang over the edge of a skyscraper, thirty-five and Kowalski are trapped onboard a rapidly sinking ship. "We filmed the underwater sequences in a huge tank," says Gross. "In all, we spent three days underwater and that part was great fun. Callum and I were given a weekend's tuition in scuba diving because I had never worn a snorkel before. It was a whole new experience for me. The story, which I co-wrote, has us stuck under the boat. The only way out of it is to strap this big welding canister to our backs upside down and to fire ourselves out. And then we have this conversation 100 feet up in the air. What seemed like a good idea at the time when you're jotting it down became this monstrous undertaking. I was up there hanging from a crane, dripping wet, crushed by a harness, for two hours in bitterly cold weather with this enormous canister strapped to my back. The harness dug into me and the whole

thing was pretty unpleasant. And I had the bruises to prove it." ▼

INUIT

AROUND ONE-THIRD OF THE (VERY SPARSE) population of the North West Territories are Inuit. Also known as Eskimo (meaning 'eaters of raw flesh'), these people of Arctic Mongolian stock now prefer to be called Inuit, meaning simply 'the people'.

Inland the Inuit hunt caribou, but their principal diet is fish and seals. The seal is a valuable resource, providing the Inuit with dog food, clothing, materials for making boats, tents and harpoon lines, as well as fuel for both light and heat. Most Inuit now live in Western housing rather than the traditional igloo, while transport is mainly by kayak or dog sled. Many earn a living from handicraft work such as soapstone carving.

According to traditional Inuit beliefs, all objects and living things have a spirit which governs every phenomenon. These natural spirits can be controlled by magical charms and talismans or by the local shaman, and the Inuit people take great care not to offend them.

As the *Due South* team discovered while filming the Pilot episode, it pays to heed local traditions and rituals (see pages 14–17 for the full story).

Top and left: Fraser does his bit to surprise a suspect in 'Seeing is Believing'. But the man who actually flew through the air was Paul Gross's stunt double.

MANHUNT

AS A CONFIRMED LESLIE NIELSEN FAN, Paul Haggis was eager to use him on *Due South*. He envisaged the actor's trademark straight-faced delivery as being ideally suited to a role of a clean-cut Mountie and decided to introduce the character in the third episode of the first season, 'Manhunt'.

"I wanted to get Leslie Nielsen on the show," says Haggis, "so when we found out that he was doing a golf video nearby, we drove out to the course to meet with him. I pitched the story and the character to him and he said, 'Sounds good.' I went home, wrote the story in three days and sent it to him. He loved it and decided to play the part. That whole episode was great fun to do."

The story centres around two old adversaries — Nielsen's character, Sgt Duncan 'Buck' Frobisher, and ruthless killer Harold Geiger. In an orgy of bloodshed, bank robber Geiger killed every cop who got close to him... except for Frobisher, who managed to bring him in alive. That was thirty years ago and now Geiger has escaped from prison. The cop killing has started all over again. The total

stands at twelve, but Geiger won't rest until he's made it thirteen by exacting revenge on Frobisher. And for the first

Above: No matter what his mode of transport, the eccentric 'Buck' remains convinced he is on horseback.

time in his long and distinguished career, Buck is running scared.

Fraser, alerted to Buck's plight by his daughter Julie, tracks him down to a Chicago hotel so grim even the rats have checked out. Confronted with a broken man, Fraser relates some of

his father's tales of Buck's bravery. "That was the man I used to be," says Buck. "Right now I'm a guy running for his life, ashamed of what he's become."

Inevitably, Fraser talks him round and the pathos gives way to comedy as the pair join forces in the pursuit of Geiger — a partnership which, for Fraser, is like teaming up with his father. They raid the bar from the Pilot film where the customers carry enough weapons to start an army and, in the best scene, visit an old folks' home. "Hands in the air!" bellows Buck to the patients, whereupon an aged man clutching a walking frame falls to the ground. Frank Drebin would have been proud of it. While Fraser is in hospital recovering from a stab wound, Haggis even manages a dig at American superiority. The nurse tells Fraser she's got a nephew in Canada. "You know him?" she asks. Fraser deems it polite to reply "Yes".

After paddling a canoe along the city sewers (in reality, a set built by the art department), Fraser, Buck and Ray surprise Geiger and his cohorts and Buck arrests him once again. The legend

Above: Once a broken man, Frobisher is reassembled by Fraser to exorcise the ghost of cold-blooded killer Harold Geiger.

lives on. A running gag in the episode is that Buck is desperate to ride a horse through the streets of Chicago but always ends up hailing a cab. In the finale, he steps into a cab bound for the airport, only to change his mind and join Fraser on horseback. Steeds rearing, they ride off down Michigan Avenue in their dress reds, leaving Ray speechless. Paul Gross admits that 'Manhunt' was a turning point for him. "I learned an enormous amount from Leslie. I remember we'd done this scene and I said to him: 'Was that any good? I feel like I blew it.' He said: 'Don't worry, it was great. You are that character. You're ninety per cent there no matter what you do.' It was actually very calming to hear that, because from that moment on I stopped feeling as nervous." ▼

"VERY NICE PEOPLE THESE AMERICANS. YOU HEAR STORIES, BUT..."

Let's hear it for DIEFENBAKER

EVERY DOG — OR INDEED, WOLF — HAS ITS DAY. SOMETIMES MORE THAN ONCE...

Right and opposite: Chinook as Diefenbaker.

IT WAS PAUL HAGGIS'S IDEA to partner Fraser with a deaf wolf. At one point, Diefenbaker was almost dropped, but has now emerged as a star in his own right. Siberian husky Draco is the fifth dog to play the part, following in the pawprints of Frankie (in the Pilot), Chinook, Kerry-Ann and, primarily, Lincoln.

Draco's trainer and coach Rick Parker says: "Draco came from a breeder in Ohio. He was only seven months old when we first saw him but it was easy to tell he had a keen and inquisitive mind. He is learning every week and as he becomes confident about his duties, new, harder commands are integrated to build up his repertoire. The only

> *"I dunno, Fraser. For some reason, wolves rarely share their inner-most thoughts with me."*

things he doesn't like are open stairs. I don't think he ever will so we minimise the need for their use. However, he tolerates them when necessary because he trusts me."

Draco has been introduced for the third season on grounds of 'production efficiency', which is a polite way of saying that some of his predecessors struggled occasionally.

David Marciano remembers a scene from the first season episode 'A Cop, a Mountie and a Baby'. "We were at an airport and it was the climax of the episode where Diefenbaker was supposed to climb up the boarding steps to the plane and then leap onto the criminal, knocking him to the ground. Well, after about fifteen takes I got tired of watching, so I started back to my trailer. Now for some reason, I decided to look back to see if Dief was going to do it this time. And I couldn't believe what I saw. There was the trainer standing off-camera with the dog in her arms about to hurl the dog at the bad guy! I don't know why I was so surprised, because this ended up becoming a common occurrence."

"Around that time," Marciano adds, "I remember going to Universal Studios with my family and watching one of their live animal shows. At one point I turned to my wife and said: 'Look how good those dogs are. Why can't our dog do that?'" ▼

Above: Diefenbaker (Draco) springs into action in the season three episode 'Asylum'.

the WILD BUNCH

EVERY DOG HAS ITS DAY, AND WITH Diefenbaker it was 'The Wild Bunch'. What actor could resist such a script? You do love scenes with the best-looking bitch in town; you get to run with the gang; you get framed for a crime you didn't commit and find yourself in a dramatic life-or-death situation; and, best of all, you get to bite your co-star. All this, and not a line to learn...

The creators of this epic and heroic role were Kathy Slevin (Paul Haggis's sister) and Jeff King. "I think that Kathy had the idea to do a story about Diefenbaker in love," remembers King, "one that included Willie, who appeared in 'Free Willie', which sounded like a great idea too. At some point we got to talking about a story that would have Diefenbaker acting in a way that would cause Fraser alarm and get them both in trouble — something to cause Fraser to examine whether keeping a wolf in a city was wrong. The animal experimentation plot came after, as we were working out the story details."

Dief has been hanging around with a group of stray mutts nicknamed the Wild Bunch, so a worried Fraser gives Willie the job of wolf-sitter. This proves a big mistake as Dief gives his minder the slip for a romantic rendezvous with Maggie, an attractive husky. When Maggie is snatched by

Above: Ray and Willie protest in vain at Diefenbaker's impending arrest.
Below: Fraser inspects the wound where Dief bit Officer Benedict.

Officer Benedict, a crooked dog catcher who is lining his own pockets by selling the neighbourhood dogs to research laboratories, Dief reacts like any suitor about to lose his loved one — he sinks his teeth into the aggressor. As a result, he is arrested and ordered to be destroyed.

Even Fraser, who is rarely without an explanation for even the strangest occurrences, is puzzled by Dief's odd behaviour. Learning that several pets in the area have gone missing, including Maggie, he reluctantly concludes that his faithful wolf has returned to his wild state. A touching scene between the pair in the dog pound is shattered when Dief, hearing Maggie's cry from another cage, leaps at Fraser and savages his arm.

As always, Fraser wants to play everything by the book — and Ray knows the very book. It is his little black book containing the names of over fifty jurors and lawmakers, several with accompanying compromising photos. There's nothing like a spot of blackmail to get a result, but for once Ray's best efforts are in vain. Dief looks doomed.

Above: 'The Wild Bunch' provides Diefenbaker with his finest hour as he strives to rescue the love of his life, Maggie.

Despite Fraser's insistence that Dief should not be sprung, Willie decides to free him in the wilds of Canada. Fearing for Willie's safety in the light of what his once trusted companion did to him, Fraser sets off in pursuit, armed with a rifle, fully prepared to destroy Diefenbaker himself rather than leave it to the authorities.

Fraser hunts him down, lines up the shot and, in the finest tradition of Westerns, takes an eternity to pull the trigger — just time enough for first Willie and then Maggie to appear and reveal the truth. Fraser abruptly turns and fires — shooting the rifle from the hands of Officer Benedict. Fittingly, the baddies are locked in a cage and Maggie, rescued by the gallant Diefenbaker, gives birth to his puppies. He did it all for love. Whaddawolf! Arnie couldn't have played it better.

"Dog wise, 'The Wild Bunch' was the most challenging shoot, apart from the Pilot," says Jeff King. "Ted Haggis [Paul's father] and Joey Young did a great job of putting together and training all the dogs. I remember during the shooting it was bitterly cold. That made it even harder. I mean, people will go out in -50°c extreme cold if you pay them. But not dogs. They are way too smart." ▼

Left: The proud father? The puppies were actually those of Kerry-Ann, one of the dogs who occasionally played Dief.

"I DON'T SEE HOW MRS PUMPUTIS' PEKINESE COULD POSSIBLY BEAR A PASSING RESEMBLANCE TO A CARIBOU, EVEN IF IT WAS WEARING SHOES."

LIEUTENANT WELSH

POSSESSED OF THE PATIENCE OF JOB, a much-feared sardonic wit and an intense loyalty to his troops, at fifty years of age Lt Welsh is coming to the stage in his career when the last thing he needs is an over-zealous Mountie riding roughshod over his command, Chicago's 27th District.

But he has to concede that Fraser and Ray do get results, even if he doesn't always understand, or approve of, their methods. For Welsh is one of the old school, believing an investigation can only be thorough if it involves a mountain of paperwork and a few ulcers.

In time he comes to warm to Fraser, to the point where he begins to regard him as one of

his men. And beneath that gruff exterior beats some form of heart. He momentarily lets his guard slip in 'All The Queen's Horses' when explaining the virtues of the RCMP's Musical Ride team to the FBI.

"It's thirty-two riders moving as one," he muses dreamily, "... perfect harmony between man and beast... a kaleidoscope of manes and tails and battle lances criss-crossing in a collage of synchronous movement. Takes your breath away..." As everyone stares at him in utter disbelief, he quickly splutters: "Hey, I was a kid. It haunted me." Normal service, though, is soon resumed.

New York-born character actor Beau Starr, who plays Lt Welsh, boasts an extensive filmography. His credits include *Halloween 5 The Revenge of Michael Myers*, *Murderous Vision*, *Dead Air*, *The November Men* and *Never Talk to Strangers*. In order to film *Due South*, he commutes to Canada from his home in California. ▼

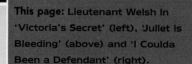

This page: Lieutenant Welsh in 'Victoria's Secret' (left), 'Juliet is Bleeding' (above) and 'I Coulda Been a Defendant' (right).

"DOG FOOD, VECCHIO?
I ASSIGNED YOU TO A DOG FOOD CASE?"

DETECTIVE JACK HUEY

ERSTWHILE PARTNER OF LOUIS Gardino and now teamed up with Thomas Dewey, Jack Huey is a highly competent detective with a built-in sense of justice. However, it's not always the kind of justice dispensed in courts of law, more a poetic justice. But that's where any similarity between Huey and Wordsworth ends. For Huey, 'a host of golden daffodils' would amount to an offensive weapon.

Huey's sometimes gung-ho attitude manifests itself most intensely in the wake of Gardino's murder. Believing gangster Frank Zuko to have been responsible for his friend's death, Huey thirsts for revenge and, when Zuko's sister Irene is accidentally killed by a stray bullet, wants Zuko framed for her murder. But Ray Vecchio is made of sterner stuff,

Above: Jack Huey was naturally distraught over the murder of his partner Gardino and was keen to exact full revenge.

and justice ultimately prevails.

Tony Craig, who plays Huey, started in showbusiness as a musician, but when his Toronto recording studio was robbed, his girlfriend decided to cheer him up by taking Craig along to a movie set to work as an extra. He ended up being offered a larger role, however, and this spawned a whole new career.

Since then, the forty-year-old Trinidadian has combined both his musical and acting skills, recording albums and appearing as a singer/drummer with artists of the calibre of Dan Hill, Etta James and Carol Pope, and acting in productions such as *Hoover vs. the Kennedys*, *The Return of Elliot Ness*, *Top Cops*, *Forever Knight*, *Scales of Justice*, *Soul Survivor*, *The Ref* and *That Old Feeling*. ▼

"MAYBE... JAZZERCISE."

DETECTIVE LOUIS GARDINO

ACCORDING TO LOUIS GARDINO, a stake-out meant a takeaway meal. For, no matter how grave the situation, Gardino's mind was never far from his stomach. Nor indeed was the rest of his body. Shortly before Gardino met an untimely end in 'Juliet is Bleeding', Ray Vecchio expressed incredulity at his colleague's ravenous appetite. "How can you still be hungry?" he asked. "You ate through half my raise!"

Known as Huey and Louie in recognition of Donald Duck's nephews, fellow detective Jack Huey and Gardino enjoyed a quick-fire station repartee with Ray... who once informed a lady caller that they were in charge of all missing cat enquiries. And Gardino was quick to defend Ray in front of Internal Affairs when Vecchio was under suspicion in 'Victoria's Secret'. "Sir," he told Lt. Welsh, "I know Vecchio's a weasel and all, but he's a straight-up cop." "You don't seriously believe that, do you?" countered the stunned Internal Affairs officer. "Oh yeah," replied Gardino straight-faced, "serious weasel."

The son of contralto Maureen Forrester and musician Eugene Kash, Montreal-born Daniel Kash trained to be an actor in England at London's Drama Centre, playing Claudius in *Hamlet*, Sam Katz in *Paradise Lost* and the title role in *King Lear*. After graduating, he appeared in a variety of stage productions in England, Canada and New York, including a season at the Stratford Festival and *A Streetcar Named Desire* (in which he played Stanley). His many television credits include *Law and Order*, *The Defenders*, *Street Legal* and *Young Indiana Jones*. Among his movie credits are a number of independent films and appearances in James Cameron's *Aliens*, *Nightbreed*, and *Gross Misconduct*. The latter was written by Paul Gross, and Kash won a Gemini nomination for best actor for his performance. Thirty-eight-year-old Kash left *Due South* in the middle of the second series in order to further his acting career in Los Angeles. ▼

Above: Between meals, Louis Gardino was a hard-working cop. His death left a hole in the force... and in Ray's car.

"SEE, THAT'S THE TROUBLE WITH SIGNS. YOU GET THE RIGHT SIGN FROM THE WRONG WOMAN, YOU END UP PAYING FOR IT THE REST OF YOUR LIFE."

ELAINE BESBRISS

As Civilian Aide at the station, Elaine Besbriss is responsible for providing the vital link between the public and the police department. Thanks to the wealth of computer information at her fingertips, Elaine is also a useful sounding-board for Fraser and Ray during the course of their investigations.

She likes her job and offers a sympathetic ear at times of stress, particularly when it comes to applying first aid to wounds on a bare-chested Fraser. She is very much the unsung heroine of the station. And while the detectives rush around grabbing all the glory, it is often Elaine's behind-the-scenes efforts which come up with the vital clue needed to crack the case.

Elaine's long suffering diligence and hard work finally come in for some long overdue recognition in the season three episode 'I Coulda Been a Defendant', in which she finally graduates.

Elaine is played by Catherine

Above: A model of diligence, Civilian Aide Elaine Besbriss has for too long been the unsung heroine of the station.

Bruhier. Raised in St John, New Brunswick, Bruhier moved to Toronto at the age of seventeen. She studied acting at the drama schools of George Brown Theatre School, York University and the University of Toronto. Soon after graduating, she won a Dora Award for her portrayal of Indira in a stage production of Carrying the Calf. On the strength of that one performance, Bruhier won the lead role of Celeste in Shaw's Transit of Venus.

She cut her television teeth as co-host on the children's series Polka Dot Door, before moving on to such shows as Knightwatch, Kung Fu: The Legend Continues, E.N.G., Top Cops and Forever Knight. She recently completed the movie Shadowbuilder.

Clearly with an eye on the future, she states that her ambition is to run her own production company. ▼

"ELAINE, WE ARE ATTEMPTING TO TRACK CRIMINALS AS THOUGH THEY ARE FUR-BEARING ANIMALS. WHAT NEWS COULD BE BAD?"

VICTORIA'S *secret*

THE TWO-HOUR 'VICTORIA'S SECRET' was a fitting finale to season one of *Due South*. Its position in the running order was no happy accident. With CBS being lobbied for renewal, it was a powerful, roller-coaster of an episode with plenty of cliffhangers to leave the audience begging for season two. Does Fraser live? Will Victoria return to haunt him? Has it finally stopped snowing?

The premise for the story had actually been drawn up right at the start of the series. Paul Haggis, who wrote and directed the episode, explains: "From the very beginning, we planned to inject some romance into the show. When Paul Gross and I were originally talking about Fraser and the show in general, we agreed that any comedy has to be based on truth. Fraser is a terrific character with one fatal flaw — he's all thumbs around women. So we started postulating: 'Why is he this

way?' We decided that there's something in Fraser's past that has made him gun-shy with the opposite sex. I thought about this for many, many months and finally came up with the idea that there was this black widow in his past. We put him in a situation where he had to choose between his love for this woman and his love for the law. I felt that having him fall in love with her and then putting her in jail was a pretty good back story for him." Haggis adds: "I wrote the whole episode in about five days."

The seeds of what was to follow were sown earlier in the series. Fraser's tragic romantic past had been hinted at more than once, and in 'You Must Remember This' he finally plucked up the courage to bare all to Ray. Unfortunately, Ray fell asleep at the vital moment and so Fraser's secret remained intact, much to the anguish of viewers who had to wait another nine weeks for the eventual denouement.

As in the Pilot epi-

Above: Behind that beautiful exterior, Victoria is a determined, ruthless criminal.

Above: The return of Victoria Metcalf brings nothing but trouble for Fraser. More than once he finds himself held at gunpoint by his old love.

sode, Paul Haggis reveals himself a master at combining high comedy with tense drama. Most of the funny stuff occurs early on. After that, the atmosphere becomes much bleaker. One of the best visual scenes sees Ray lovingly setting up a pool table in his dining room. Having taken great care to ensure that the table is level and that there is just about enough elbow room to play shots, he racks the balls. Come the moment of truth, he removes the triangle... and all the balls roll to one side of the table. Back to the drawing board.

A recurring theme in *Due South* is the unhelpful hotel desk clerk. The general impression is that they won't tell you what day it is unless they are paid for their trouble. Here, Ray and Fraser call in on a typically seedy hotel in search of Victoria's accomplice, Jolly. The clerk, wearing the world's thickest glasses (indeed, most microscopes have slimmer lenses), is shown Jolly's photo. He pulls it to within half

an inch of his nose but insists he doesn't know him. Ray tries again. Same photo. Same response. "So how about this guy?" asks Ray, showing him the same photo for a third time. The clerk recognises him immediately and gives the room number. As a nice touch, he then wipes the camera lens with a cloth.

The skeleton in Fraser's cupboard dates back to an Alaskan bank robbery eight years earlier. One raider died, another went south and the third, a woman, fled across the Canadian border in a light plane

"SHE'S, YOU KNOW... CANADIAN."

before being forced down by bad weather. Fraser tracked her to a forlorn spot called Fortitude Pass. She was almost frozen and close to death, but Fraser wrapped his body around hers to keep her warm as a vicious storm closed in. Then, when he began to slip away, it was her turn to save him by reciting a poem over and over. Forced together by circumstance, they grew closer by the minute. Fraser found his pack and they gorged themselves, relieved to be alive. After five nights together, they neared civilisation and she asked him to let her go. The police didn't even know that he had found her, nor did they know her name, but he knew that he had to turn her in. Since then he has been haunted by the image of Victoria Metcalf.

Despite assurances from his father's ghost that he did the right thing, Fraser remains racked with guilt and so, when he suddenly spots Victoria in Chicago, he has to talk to her. She doesn't make it easy for him, but before long they rekindle their lost love and tumble into bed amidst a maelstrom of emotions, the scenes acquiring extra poignancy by being played out to two backing tracks from Sarah McLachlan — 'Possession' and

'Fumbling Towards Ecstasy'. But any joy is short-lived. For Victoria has been followed to Chicago by her old partner, the inappropriately-named Jolly, who

Above: Victoria won't let anyone stand in her way — including Fraser.
Below: Fraser lies on the platform, accidentally gunned down by Ray.

reckons she has half a million dollars belonging to him from the bank robbery. He wants his money back and the first to pay the price is Dief, shot while defending Fraser's apartment.

Jolly is closing in fast on Victoria. Fraser tracks him to a downtown zoo (in reality Toronto Zoo) where, after a knife fight watched by an inquisitive crocodile, Jolly escapes — but only as far as his car, where the waiting Victoria shoots him in cold blood. She later tells Fraser it was self defence, but then does a vanishing act, leaving him to take the rap for the killing. To make matters worse, it emerges that the money Fraser and Ray have been spending recently came from the Alaskan bank job and the bullet which killed Jolly came from the gun used to shoot Dief — a thirty-eight, the same calibre as Fraser's. To put the final nail in Fraser and Ray's coffin, it seems that Victoria Metcalf died in a car smash two months previously. Everything points to Fraser having shot Jolly, especially when his gun is recovered from the polar bear pool. The world's favourite Mountie is charged with first degree murder.

Released on bail (put together by Ray), Fraser gets a call from Victoria. They meet in the back of an X-rated book store — the only time Fraser has ever been near such an establishment — where she reveals that the girl who died in the crash was her sister who

"YOU HAVE A WOMAN
IN THERE???"

Above and previous page: Victoria prepares to seduce Fraser by wearing his Mountie uniform. At least she left the hat off.

Below: His well ordered mind for
once in a turmoil, Fraser considers
giving up everything for Victoria.

"WELL... I DO HAVE
SOMETHING LIKE EIGHTY-TWO
SICK DAYS COMING TO ME."

had borrowed her car. The police simply assumed that the dead girl was Victoria. With his usually ordered mind already in a turmoil, Fraser is thrown into even further confusion when Victoria announces that she wants him to run away with her.

The climax is a fast-moving blend of plot and counter-plot, culminating in diamonds and dollar bills being scattered over the train station platform while Victoria makes her escape. Even when she realises Fraser has tricked her, she still wants him to flee with her. She holds out her hand from the moving train to Fraser running along the platform; Ray thinks she's about to shoot Fraser; Ray fires his gun; the bullet hits Fraser; Fraser sinks to the floor and tells Ray, "I was going with her"; Fraser recites a poem as Victoria disappears into the distance.

Would Fraser really have allowed his heart to rule his head and gone off with Victoria? Short of season four and a return appearance by Victoria, I guess we'll never know. ▼

due
SOUTH

season TWO

EYES WIDE
open

deaf EARS, loud VOICES

SEASON TWO GETS UNDERWAY...
BUT NOT WITHOUT A STRUGGLE

THE FIRST EVER CANADIAN-produced series to be screened prime time on one of the three big American networks, *Due South* became an instant hit for CBS. Despite being scheduled opposite *Friends* and *Mad About You*, the first episode reached a highly respectable fourteenth in the national ratings. The show earned rave reviews and seemed set for a long life, but in the second half of the season CBS started shuffling *Due South* in the schedules and the ratings suffered accordingly. "I just think we needed a better time slot," reflects Paul Haggis. "I got no negative feedback about the show. All I heard was: 'We don't know your show — we don't know when you're on.'"

Nevertheless, *Due South* was a big success in its native Canada, where it was the fifth highest-rated series overall and won no fewer than four Gemini awards. The series also proved popular with American critics.

USA Today wrote: "This quietly hip, subtly smart series could be a good fit for a new and improved CBS. If *Due South* doesn't get the renewal it deserves, that would be a shame, a lost opportunity." The words fell on deaf ears. Even though *Due South*'s final ratings position of fifty-second in America was thirteen places higher than Fox's *The X-Files*, CBS announced

that it would not be taking a second series. *Due South* was cancelled.

But Canadian broadcasters were reluctant to let such a fine series die, particularly since it had also attracted a sizeable following in Britain, Europe and Australia. In July 1995, Alliance Communications and CTV, *Due South*'s Canadian broadcaster, came up with

> "*Vecchio, are you familiar with that old Spanish expression 'el guardia del traffico'...?*"

Above: Grand injustice! Fraser campaigns for the renewal of *Due South*. Okay, okay... it's a scene from 'One Good Man'.

more cash and this, allied to additional government funding, enabled *Due South* to be renewed for a second season, regardless of the lack of commitment

from CBS. In fact, by the time CBS did finally commit, Alliance and CTV had already produced eight episodes of season two. Arthur Weinthal, CTV's vice-president of programming, commented: "We all had a growing resolve that this is a show that Canadians quite clearly like... that is one of the best things we've ever done in this country, and we just have to make an effort to keep something worthwhile going."

In the event, CBS buckled in the face of sustained fan power. Ann Keitz, a *Due South* devotee based in Washington, DC, began a letter-writing campaign, targeting sponsors and critics, with the result that CBS picked the series up mid-season.

Without CBS funding, the budget for the second season of *Due South* had to be reduced, but Paul Gross saw this as no bad thing. "The core of the show is the relationship between Fraser and Ray," he told *TV Guide* in November 1995. "The thing I enjoy most is the banter and interaction. With the reduced budgets, we're going to have to concentrate on that more this year."

The principal change to the second season was behind the scenes. When it appeared that *Due South* would not be renewed, Paul Haggis began work on an ill-fated drama series called *EZ Streets*. When *Due South* was suddenly picked up again, Haggis stepped down as the show's executive producer but continued as creative consultant.

NORTH

BOTH PAUL GROSS AND DAVID MARCIANO name 'North', the opener to season two, as one of their favourite *Due South* episodes. The story sees Fraser and Ray stranded in the wilds following a plane crash, and being stalked through the woods by a killer. It was filmed at a picturesque spot called Elora Gorge, about one and a half hours north west of Toronto.

Jeff King, who wrote 'North', says: "I took the four characters — Fraser, Ray and the spirits of their two dead fathers — and pitted them against an unseen protagonist. There is an underlying theme in that episode which is that our greatest adversaries are the ones that are inside us. So I subtitled it 'I Never Camped With My Father', which was Ray's thing to overcome. I put our heroes in a situation which was opposite to the one in Chicago, in that Ray becomes the fish out of water and Fraser is put back in his natural element. Unfortunately for Fraser, he's injured and blinded. Even though he can't see, he's still behaving just like a guy who knows exactly what he's doing and can get himself and Ray out of their situation. But it's Ray who ends up saving them both."

Above: Ending with a bang? In 'Red, White or Blue' Fraser and Ray must defuse a bomb due to go off if their combined heart rates exceed 200 beats per minute.

His place at the helm was taken by Jeff King and Kathy Slevin, and David Marciano was quick to seize the opportunity. "They were more open to my suggestions and what I needed to make the character sing," remembers Marciano. "There were things about Ray that didn't make sense. No cop of fifteen years would do some of the things Ray did. If he did, he'd be dead. So I kept fighting for him to be more intelligent. Jeff and Kathy heard me loud and clear, and we were able to make changes which allowed Ray to become someone with a big heart, a good friend and a complete police officer. All the things I couldn't get done in season one we were able to do in season two. I'm very happy about that because it was successful for me as well as the character." ▼

bird IN THE HAND

THE CREATORS OF *DUE SOUTH* DON'T believe in allowing good characters to go to waste. Visitors such as veteran Mountie 'Buck' Frobisher, pickpocket Willie Lambert, gangster Frank Zuko and compulsive liar Ian Mac-Donald all returned in later episodes, a tactic which also heightens the sense of continuity in the show. Thus Gerrard, the villain of the piece in the Pilot, comes back to haunt Fraser in Paul Haggis's 'Bird in the Hand'.

It is essentially a dark episode with Fraser trying to come to terms with the task of safeguarding his father's killer. But, in true Haggis fashion, there are a few lighter moments, courtesy of the Canadian consulate's young Temporary Assistant Interim Associate Deputy Liaison Officer, Constable Renfield Turnbull, living proof that length of title is no guarantee of intelligence. Turnbull's enthusiasm is certainly infectious, but so was the plague. He merely succeeds in complicating the simplest task with an obsessive dedication which makes Fraser look positively indifferent.

Gerrard is serving a life sentence for his part in the murder of Fraser Sr.

The story is that he has agreed to testify against an American arms dealer called Lloyd Nash in the hope

Above: Ray and Fraser prepare to scour Chicago for Gerrard.
Below: Fraser acts as peacemaker between Ray and Lloyd Nash.

of securing an early release but, brought to Chicago for the trial, he has given two US marshals the slip at O'Hare Airport. ATF (Department of

Alcohol, Tobacco and Firearms) Agent McFadden and FBI Agent Borland are keen to ascertain his whereabouts... and that's where Fraser comes in.

Fraser soon finds Gerrard and hauls him back to the consulate where Fraser Sr. suggests retribution. "Think of it as a son's gift to his father," he urges. "You did forget my birthday." "You were dead," counters Fraser.

The old man has the perfect solution — death by desk lamp. "We'll crack his skull and make it look like a freak lighting accident — happens all the time. Lightning strikes the wires, sends a jolt through the line, the lamp hops up, hits him in the skull, splits it in two and you never had the chance to prevent it, happens so fast."

But Fraser has no intention of carrying out his father's wishes or of handing Gerrard over to the agents. This proves a wise move as it emerges that Gerrard is not testifying against Nash but against ATF agents who are involved in gun smuggling. And McFadden is the ringleader. With McFadden about to silence Gerrard,

Below: Can't work on an empty stomach. Ray finds that a ready supply of doughnuts helps to fuel the brain.

> "NO, HE APPRECIATES YOUR TIME. I DON'T APPRECIATE ANYTHING."

GERRARD

ON THE FACE OF IT, CHIEF SUPERINtendent Gerrard of the RCMP is as straight as a Roman road. But in reality, he's as crooked as a Roman nose. Gerrard was in the pay of a mighty hydro-electric plant, hushing up how they had flooded the land, killing hundreds of caribou. When Fraser Sr. threatened to expose everything, Gerrard had his friend and colleague killed.

Consequently Gerrard represents the two things that Fraser detests above all else — a corrupt Mountie and the murderer of his father. So when Fraser has to protect Gerrard from a gang of gun smugglers, against whom Gerrard is about to testify, it requires all of the Mountie's legendary devotion to duty. Fraser simply refuses to allow personal emotions to cloud his judgement and vows to deliver Gerrard safely to court.

And while the gloating Gerrard knows that Fraser's ethics mean that he will guard him with his life, the ghost of Fraser Sr. is less diplomatic. "Shoot him, son," he orders. "Shoot him between his rat-like little eyes."

Fraser and Ray permanently, Fraser employs characteristically inventive diversionary tactics.

To everyone's acute embarrassment, he embarks on a slushy speech about how he had always seen Gerrard as a father figure. McFadden momentarily drops his guard, allowing Fraser to hurl a knife into the barrel of the agent's gun. Dodging bullets,

Fraser explains his thinking to Ray: "We needed an advantage so I had to unnerve them. And there's nothing more unnerving to men than talking about feelings."

Gerrard tries to escape through a third-floor window but is left hanging on to the sill by his fingertips. He sees the ghost of Fraser Sr. at the window offering his hand. Gerrard reaches out

but there is no one there and the bent Mountie crashes to the ground where he is duly arrested.

It might not have been quite the revenge Bob Fraser had in mind, but it's a start. ▼

> "GOOD DOG. BITE HIM AGAIN."

lines of LATITUDE

THE POPULARITY OF *DUE SOUTH* SPEAKS FOR ITSELF — LITERALLY

Above: 'Pizzas and Promises'. Would you buy a used car from this man?

THE CONSISTENTLY HIGH standard of sharp and witty dialogue, combined with a freedom to liberally parody both Canadians and Americans, has produced enough choice quotes — or, as fans refer to them, 'Duesies' — to fill a book. Or, in this case, two pages.

MOTHER: He's very nice, so polite.
RAY: He's Canadian, Mom.
MOTHER: Oh. I thought he was just sick or something.
('the Pilot')

FRASER (to Dief): Stay here.
RAY: He reads lips?
FRASER: I've never been sure. If so, he's self-taught.
('the Pilot')

RAY: You know, we just took out seven guys. One more and you qualify for American citizenship.
('the Pilot')

FRASER: I need your help, Ray.
RAY: Does it involve domestic animals?
FRASER: Not that I'm aware.
RAY: Then I'm your man.
('Manhunt')

FRASER: These last two blocks. I've been tracking a Lhasa Apso.
RAY: You've been tracking a *Lhasa Apso*??
FRASER: I know. If word of this ever gets back to the Territories, I'll never live it down.

RAY: Mounties can be so cruel.
('Pizzas and Promises')

FRASER: When I was a young scout, working on my ecology badge, I insinuated myself into a hunting party in order to catch a baby seal killer.
RAY: So, what happened?

Above: 'Gift of the Wheelman'.

FRASER: Well, I was clubbed repeatedly, Ray.
('Pizzas and Promises')

GARDINO: We believe that the perpetrators were dressed in Santa Claus suits in order to facilitate their getaway by blending into the crowd.
WELSH: In that people don't usually notice armed men fleeing a crime scene in big red suits.
('Gift of the Wheelman')

ELAINE: Sure. But she called from her car. It was a cell phone.
HUEY: No, you're never going to track a cell, it's a nightmare.
FRASER: Not really. Not if you've tracked a caribou.
('You Must Remember This')

FRASER: Also, sir, I think you'll be pleased to know that I've taken the liberty of officially reprimanding myself.
WELSH: Good, good. Put it in the file with the rest of them. Get out of my office.
('An Eye for an Eye')

ELAINE: I always wanted a pair of ruby slippers. I used to try on my mother's high heels, standing in front of the mirror, click my heels together and say 'there's no place like home...'
GARDINO: Me too.
('The Deal')

Left: Fraser and his father discuss the finer points of hats in 'Victoria's Secret'.

FRASER: You know, we had a schoolyard bully in Tuktoyaktuk, once. Sometimes at night I can still remember him... coming into the classroom swinging that otter over his head. There was just no reasoning with him.
RAY: And I thought we had nothing in common.
('The Deal')

FRASER: What's wrong with your hat, Dad?
FRASER SR.: It's the one they buried me in. They had to snip off the back so that I'd lie flat. I'm sure they meant well, but they don't realise how embarrassing these things can be in the afterlife.
('Victoria's Secret')

THATCHER: I don't dislike animals, Fraser. I've had pets.
FRASER: Really.
THATCHER: Small ones. A dachshund.
FRASER: Oh.
THATCHER: It died.
('The Promise')

FRASER: He later sold the masks to two separate countries and they've finally been reunited after more than 100 years.
RAY: So... ?
FRASER: It's an important moment in history for both Canada and France, not to mention the political, cultural and religious significance it holds for the North American people.
RAY: And... ?

FRASER: Worth over a million dollars.
RAY: Oh, now you're talking.
('Mask')

THATCHER: We will speak only when spoken to. We will keep our responses short and to the point. We will maintain our postures and above all — we will act naturally.
THATCHER: Why are they staring at me?
FRASER: I suspect they're terrified, ma'am.
('All The Queen's Horses')

THATCHER: You ran into a burning building to save a mohair sweater.
FRASER: Yes, sir.
THATCHER: Well, pardon me if that sounds like sheer stupidity.
FRASER: Yes, sir.
THATCHER: You don't agree?
FRASER: No, sir. Stupidity would have been if I'd gone back in for your leather chaps.
('The Witness')

RAY: You're off duty and unless someone shot a moose you don't have jurisdiction.
('White Men Can't Jump to Conclusions')

RAY: Oh, you're the most irritating man in the world.
FRASER: Define irritating.
RAY: Well, no, you look it up Mr Encyclopedia.
FRASER: Well, I think you mean Mr Dictionary, don't you?
('Red, White or Blue') ▼

Above: 'The Witness'.

Juliet IS BLEEDING

'THE DEAL' FROM THE FIRST SEASON IS one of David Marciano's favourite episodes. It does for Ray Vecchio what 'Victoria's Secret' does for Fraser — it gives him a history, an old flame, and a skeleton in the cupboard. Ray's long-lost love is Irene Zuko, sister of Ray's old school rival, Frank Zuko, now one of the city's major mobsters. She is a decent woman but, because of her family connections, a dangerous one to know... as Ray discovers in one of the darkest of all *Due South* episodes, 'Juliet Is Bleeding'.

Jeff King, who penned the episode with Kathy Slevin, says: "We wanted to do a story about Ray and an old flame who he is reunited with — something that would take him back to the old neighbourhood and that would put him opposite Zuko again. We were trying to do a good story for David's character."

He continues: "There was also another consideration. Daniel Kash, who played Detective Louis Gardino, had wanted to leave the show. We had made a commitment to Danny to let him go by a certain date and so we killed his character in 'Juliet'."

Ray, Fraser, Huey and Louis are out on the town celebrating Ray's promotion to Detective First Grade. They choose the Villa Borghese restaurant

Above: Ray proves unwelcome at the birthday party of Frank Zuko. **Below:** The hapless Gardino prepares to get into Ray's car.

in Little Italy — one of the few able to cater for Gardino's voracious appetite. To Ray's discomfort, there is another party at the restaurant that night — Frank Zuko's birthday party

— and among their number is Ray's childhood sweetheart, Irene.

As the evening progresses, Ray becomes bolder and asks Irene to dance. Zuko barely conceals his anger. But the gangster is about to have weightier things on his mind. For his trusted lieutenant, Michael Sorrento, is intent on seizing control of the Zuko crime empire and decides the best way to get Frankie out of the way is to have him framed for murder — Ray's murder. Sorrento arranges for a bomb to be planted on the Riv, but the plan goes wrong when Gardino, on a whim, chooses to take Ray's car for a spin. He turns the key in the ignition and the car explodes, killing him instantly.

Ray is certain that Zuko was behind the bombing. Huey wants to avenge his dead partner by taking down Zuko once and for all, by fair means or foul. Fraser prefers to play things by the book, particularly since he is convinced of Zuko's innocence.

When detonators are discovered under the floorboards in the tool shed at Zuko's mansion, Zuko is arrested. But Fraser remains sceptical — among other things, why would Zuko keep

detonators in his own house, just yards from his daughter's bedroom window? And why, if he was guilty, hadn't he arranged a watertight alibi?

Ray doesn't want to know and pours scorn on all of Fraser's misgivings: "Who the hell do you think died out there, huh? So you've got a wire that should be melted, but it's not? You've got an absence of finger stains, you've got Zuko without an alibi, when he should have one. All right, maybe someone did plant those detonators, and maybe they didn't. All I know is that we've got a dead cop — a friend, and we've got the guy who did it. Do you follow me?"

In the wake of Gardino's funeral, Ray calls on Irene by scrambling up a vine outside her bedroom window. Although he looks like something the cat dragged in, she receives him warmly. They chat about old times but the conversation quickly switches to her brother. Irene is torn between the two men and fears that, because of her, they will end up killing each other. Meanwhile, Fraser has secured Zuko's release — a young neighbour having confirmed that Zuko was at home at the time of the bombing. Furthermore, Fraser has identified the platinum cigar clipper used to cut the wire as belonging to Michael Sorrento. The Mountie confronts Sorrento with the evidence and tells him the news he doesn't want to hear... that Zuko is out.

Betrayed from within, Zuko is near breaking point. So when he sees that Irene has packed her bags, ready to

"OKAY, SO I BELTED HIM — BUT HE PUSHED ME FIRST."

run off with Ray, it is too much for him. With Sorrento, Ray, Fraser and half of the Chicago Police Department arriving at Zuko's mansion, a gun battle starts. When the smoke dies down, it's not Ray, Zuko or Sorrento lying bleeding on the floor — it is Irene, hit by a stray bullet. Ray and Zuko have lost the one person they both loved.

The vengeful Huey wants Ray to say Zuko shot Irene deliberately, but though Ray is torn, he remembers the only thing Irene ever asked of him — not to allow his revenge to destroy both of them. In her memory, he honours her wish and with heavy heart lets his enemy walk away.

Looking back, Jeff King has mixed feelings about Gardino's sudden and tragic exit. "With hindsight, I wish we had done it in a different way. Louis' death put a pall on the episode that was hard to relieve. It made the story more harrowing than I think even we thought it would turn out to be. Don't get me wrong, I love the story and it's a really great episode. But it was very, very harrowing. A bit of a departure."

Paul Gross certainly shares this view. "One of the most difficult things for us back then was finding a consistent tone," he recalls. "We'd go from something as dark and bleak as 'Juliet Is Bleeding' to something very light and goofy with a guy who believes that he's talking to aliens. I think we definitely needed to identify those things which gave the show its particular style and should have tried to stick with them a bit more vigorously." ▼

Opposite left: Ray with his old flame Irene Zuko, played by actress Carrie-Anne Moss.

FRANK ZUKO

FRANK ZUKO AND RAY VECCHIO GO BACK a long way. To the school playground to be precise, where Ray could only look on helplessly as his friend was beaten to a pulp by the bullying Zuko. Twenty years on, and Frank Zuko is still a bully. Except that now he wears sharp suits instead of a blazer and shorts and the tools of his trade have progressed from catapults and knuckle-dusters to guns and knives.

Frank Zuko is a gangster, and a particularly nasty one at that. Outwardly, he's Mr. Respectable — big house, doting family — but that's only because he always gets his team of hired thugs to carry out his dirty work. Ray became a cop partly because he was brought up on the mean streets and so knew how the criminal mind worked, partly to spite his cop-hating father and partly to rid the world of scum like Zuko.

So when the two men renew their acquaintance in 'The Deal', Ray seizes the opportunity to atone for his schoolyard cowardice and humiliates Zuko in a one-on-one fight. To salvage his hard-man reputation, Zuko is forced to make a deal and call off a hit on shoemaker Joey Paducci. But Zuko is not one to forgive and forget. Ray knows he could be living on borrowed time.

"YOU SEE THIS? THIS COMES WITH A GUN — NOW DO WE GET DESSERT?"

A GOOD MAN
is hard to find

PAUL GROSS ON HUMAN NATURE, AND GETTING BACK TO NATURE

PAUL GROSS NEVER QUITE knows what to expect when he opens the pile of fan mail which arrives on his desk each week. "Most of it is very sweet," says Gross, "but some of it is pretty weird. I got one letter from a woman saying it's so nice to write to you and I love your show and you have rekindled feelings in me that I haven't experienced in some time. And then it goes on for two pages of absolutely graphic description of what she would like to do to me, concluding by saying that for your information, I'm an eighty-six-year-old woman living in a retirement home in California! She enclosed a pair of her underwear. I wasn't clear how I should respond...

"Another time, someone sent a tapestry of me in full Mountie uniform, in bed beside a woman in a nightie. The words '*Due South* — Sweet Dreams' had been sewn to the border. It was a lovely gift, but I wasn't sure what to do with it."

While not entirely comfortable with his status as a sex symbol, Gross can see why his character has appeal. "I also get letters from wronged women who say a good man is hard to find," he muses. "There's something very appealing about Fraser's goodness. I don't think there's a human being like him — certainly I've never met one — but actually the stuff he believes in is pretty

simple. Try to be nice, have some manners, help people out. It's a sad comment on our times that he's viewed as some kind of freak, that honest and moral is odd."

Gross admits that Fraser is a tough act to live up to and that when he initially read the script he had no idea

> ## *"I thought I was in love once. And then, later, I thought it was just an inner ear imbalance..."*

Above: Fraser embarks on another Inuit tale. Ray tries to look interested.

how to play the character. "And then," he remembers, "the first day on the set, I put on the uniform. The jacket is

about four inches thick and so stiff that you've got to stand straight or you'd decapitate yourself. And I thought, I see, he's upright — in every definition of the word."

Gross is blessed with a well developed, even wicked, sense of humour and is philosophical about stories that Diefenbaker used to receive as much, if not more, fan mail than him. He has little choice since his own daughter is one of Diefenbaker's biggest fans and used to insist that Gross be Fraser at home so that she could be Diefenbaker.

He explains: "I would get back after an eighteen-hour day to be met by Hannah, who would pretend that she was a dog by crawling on her hands and knees and then insisting on licking my arms. We are upstaged by the dog — it's a fact. They say in the States that a dog is equivalent to between three and five [audience] share points. For some reason people just turn it on. I don't know whether the dog still gets as much fan mail as me — they've stopped telling me..."

Family life is all-important to Gross, as is the great outdoors, and he enjoys nothing more than getting away from the pressures of work by heading off into the Rocky Mountains.

"When I'm not working I try to get away from Toronto," he says. "I like the space. Film sets are crowded and you get no privacy. It's nice just to dis-

appear. It can be tricky though. I've been bitten by a rattlesnake, but it didn't get through my boot. And I fell over a black bear once when I was about seventeen. I was running down this trail at twilight and I tripped over something which I thought was a root, but turned out to be a bear. I looked back to see the bear turn, flop its head over and gaze at me. I stared at the bear

Above: She got her man. Fraser escorts diplomat's daughter Christina Nichols to the Consulate party in 'Chicago Holiday'.

Above: 'The Promise'. Left and right: Getting the last word. Paul Gross considers the reasons for the success of *Due South*, but strangely Diefenbaker has no comment.

thinking, 'This is going to be awful', but he just went back to sleep. It's a real blow to your ego, actually. Well, why don't you want to maul me?"

Fishing is another one of Gross's passions, and he remembers a particularly worrying incident while shark fishing off the coast of California. "I was fishing away and they're sort of like big catfish. There's no fight. I was talking to one of the guys, telling him I was a bit disappointed that they didn't fight more, when the boat suddenly went up on a swell, the fish gave an almighty tug and I went flying overboard, still holding the rod.

"The thing is that fifteen minutes earlier I had asked the captain of the charter boat, 'How much are these fishing rods?' And they were about $500 each. So the only thought in my head was: 'Don't lose the guy's rod.' So the shark's going down and I wouldn't let go of the stupid thing. I reckon the shark thought, 'It's not enough that you've stuck a hook in my mouth, you're coming down to get me!' The shark surfaced and I popped up at the

same time. They all said they'd never seen a face as purely terrified as mine.

"They backed the boat off and I got in, still clutching the fishing rod, and managed to land the shark. The next

Above: Paul Gross (as Fraser) speaks out... and out... and out... in the Frank Capra inspired 'One Good Man'.

day I had a bruise that went from the top of my thigh to my knee. That was my shark fishing expedition."

Paul Gross describes *Due South* as an 'urban fable'. Why does he think it has been so successful? "The relationship between the characters is extraordinarily important," explains Gross. "Fraser is a unique character to television and because of him the show has a kind of generosity at its core that is lacking in most programmes and is viewed nostalgically by the audience. People are tired of cynicism. So if a hero comes along who can lead the way through decency and honesty, people grab on to him.

"I think it's irrelevant to Americans that Fraser is from Canada. He could just as easily be Norwegian. There's that strain in America of the heroic figure who drops in from another planet... And to Americans, Canada is another planet. But Fraser gives the show a generous heart and I think that's part of its appeal.

"Either that," he adds, "or it's just the dog!" ▼

RCW 139

ONE OF THE MANY MYSTERIES ABOUT *Due South* surrounds the vehicle licence plate RCW 139. Just one of a pool of plates assigned to the show, it was quickly spotted by many eagle-eyed viewers as being attached to different vehicles in different episodes. At first, the duplication was accidental, but now the plate has become an in-joke and regularly appears on background vehicles.

Such is the number's fame that it was adopted by The Friends of *Due South*, an on-line chat group of 800 worldwide fans, for the title of their first three-day convention in Toronto in August 1996. The convention was so successful that it was repeated the following year and 15 August 1997 was officially declared 'Friends of *Due South* Day'.

Over 1,500 fans converged on Toronto from as far afield as Denmark, Australia and Britain to meet Paul Gross, Callum Keith Rennie and, of course, Diefenbaker. Events included a wolf-howling competition and a stuffed otter toss.

Left: Fraser is left holding the baby. A scene from 'A Cop, a Mountie and a Baby'.

a RAY *of* HOPE

DAVID MARCIANO RINGS THE CHANGES FOR *DUE SOUTH*

Right: In 'An Invitation to Romance', Ray's offer of help goes beyond the call of duty...

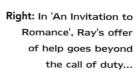

DAVID MARCIANO FREELY admits that working on *Due South* was not always a bed of roses. "The best way to describe season one was pugnacious," he says. "I had reservations about certain aspects of the character right from the start. I thought that no cop of fifteen years would do some of the things Ray did. If he did, he'd be dead. I thought he should be more intelligent, more honest, hipper. But the changes I asked for were not addressed.

"So that's when I took my stand for the betterment of Ray," explains Marciano, "and that fight continued all the way through to episode seventeen, 'The Deal'. Kathy Slevin and I got into it pretty hard and we both broke down. We were both fighting the same fight... Someone had finally heard me and Ray blossomed from there."

Judging from Marciano's initial reluctance to take the part of Ray, it's clear the character grew both on and with him. "I think the way Ray's character has developed fits in with how someone like him would change because of Fraser's influence," he explains. "The inclination, when you're comparing yourself to someone so perfect, is to look at your own imperfections. You start to feel a little inferior, a little insecure, then you realise your character also has good qualities. Ray is very loyal, he's brave and he's clever in his own way. He can be brash but he has a very generous heart."

Marciano continues: "Fraser and Ray are both hungry for friendship, though they're both loners. Fraser is alone in a big city after coming from the country. And though Ray has his family,

"Fraser, this is Armani!"

Above: David Marciano acts, Paul Gross does his level best not to react.

he is a bit of a loner too. And that's what first brought them together."

A quieter man than his screen character, Marciano nevertheless talks with intense passion about the rel-ationship between Fraser and Ray: "*Due South* was Benny and Ray. It was that special relationship that only two people who love each other in their hearts have. *Due South* is two co-workers who became friends out of adversity... friends who were willing to give up each other's lives in order to save one another for the good of humanity."

Marciano also resisted att-empts to spice up the show: "There was pressure from the American networks to beef it up with *NYPD Blue* levels of nudity, violence and profanity. But we fought it. If we had given in, we'd have been no different to any other show. We had to keep our integrity and stay different."

In spite of his character problems during the first sea-son, Marciano's keen eye for the absurd did not desert him. "One of the most memorable mom-ents took place on the first day of shooting. The first scene in 'Free Willie' shows the young man who played Willie, Paul Gross, Diefenbaker and myself. The dog we had wasn't the one from the Pilot, and we had never worked with him before. The director said, 'Action!' and the dog just bolted and ran. The director yelled, 'Cut! Somebody get the dog!' So they got the dog and we got ready to try again. In that scene I had to throw over a garbage can while yelling at Willie. The dog stop-

Above: David Marciano fought tooth and nail to make Ray Vecchio a more realistic cop and character. In season two his persistence was finally rewarded.

ped in front of the can, lifted up his leg, relieved himself and then left the scene. We couldn't believe what was happening. Those were the first two takes we did of the *Due South* series..."

"My most difficult scene was in the Pilot," recalls Marciano, "at the end, where I'm talking to Fraser while he's on duty outside the consulate. He's just standing there looking straight ahead. There was little to work off. For me," Marciano continues, "it's one of the hardest scenes to do as an actor, because acting is reacting. The most important tool I have as an actor is my ears, so if my scene partner isn't saying anything, for the most part I'm doing all the work. It can be frustrating, which of course worked for that scene."

Although only currently scheduled to appear in one or two episodes of season three, Marciano is busier than ever before. "My wife and I are working on her screenplay, *Needles*, which we hope to get produced by the summer of '98 and I am scheduled to reprise my role as Giorgio, the Don's eldest son, in *The Last Don II*. Plus I'm doing some work with a new director. It's a very exciting time." ▼

Above: A scene from 'North', one of Marciano's favourite episodes.

SOME LIKE IT *red*

SOME THINGS REALLY JUST DON'T BEAR thinking about. Dr Niles Crane in dungarees. Andy Sipowicz in lycra. A Mountie in drag. Yet, in 'Some Like It Red', a homage to the Jack Lemmon/Tony Curtis movie *Some Like It Hot*, our hero Fraser dons a red wig (once he's remembered to remove the tag) and a pair of high heels to assume the guise of Ms Fraser, art teacher at a Catholic girls school.

With his broad shoulders, deep voice and long legs, Fraser as a woman could best be described as imposing, a cross between Cindy Crawford and a linebacker. Not only do Welsh, Huey, Elaine and Ray not recognise this Amazonian figure when 'she' first glides through the station, but the first two take a positive shine to her. This marks them down not only as being lousy detectives but also as having highly dubious taste in women.

Fraser takes on this bizarre undercover assignment in order to trace Celine, a runaway student at the convent school where Ray's eighth-grade

sweetheart is now Sister Anne, nun and headmistress. (She and Ray must have gone to wildly different careers advice sessions.)

After agonising over whether teal or mustard is his colour, Fraser slips effortlessly into his new gender, and nearly forgets to remove his earrings when changing back into his Mountie uniform. Ms Fraser is soon dispensing

invaluable advice to her charges. "It takes seven fewer muscles to smile than it does to frown," she tells Celine's troubled roommate Melissa. "Save your energy. You're gonna need it in your child-bearing years." Later, Ms Fraser trots out a typically Fraser-like homily from the far north about how it wasn't always the prettiest girls who were the most popular — it was the girls with the sharpest teeth because they were handy for cutting leather! This is scarcely a comfort to Melissa.

When Fraser discovers a flask engraved with the name of Frank Nitti, Al Capone's right hand man, to go with the earlier discovery of Eliot Ness's gun, Ray is dumbfounded. "What is this? A garage sale for *The Untouchables*?" It is Ray's oddball uncle Lorenzo, who still thinks he's living in the days of Prohibition, who solves the mystery by revealing details of a secret vault built by the mob on the school grounds back in 1931.

The action switches to the school dance where

Above: There's nothing worse than having a gun pointed at your head... particularly when you've just done your hair.

Above: Bearing a somewhat unsettling resemblance to Frida from Abba, Ms Fraser trips the light fantastic with Ray.

Ms Fraser ends up dancing with a male teacher who sees himself as a latter-day Travolta and drools: "You can really move for a big woman." Just when her newfound admirer is about to make a move on her, Ray — to Fraser's intense relief —steps in and commandeers Ms Fraser for the next dance. They certainly make a lovely couple.

Fraser and Ray find Celine and round up the gang trying to loot the vault. But there is one final shock for Fraser... and Melissa. As he dives to catch a precious bottle of vintage scotch, his wig flies off. Melissa is horrified. "Oh, my God, Ms Fraser. You're a cross-dresser!" There's just

Above: Paul Gross found dressing up as a woman to be both hard work and an extremely painful experience.

no fooling some people.

Judging by Paul Gross's reaction to the episode, it seems highly unlikely that Fraser will be slipping into stockings and suspenders in the future. "Dressing up as a woman was hard work," Gross laments, "but I think every man should dress up in women's clothing once for a little insight into what they go through. The worst we have is ties! The women's shoes were painful and the corset I wore made it difficult to breathe. The foundation garments women have to wear are terrible. Whoever invented brassieres, girdles and nylons most surely was a descendant of the Marquis de Sade!" ▼

"JUST GET IN THE CAR BEFORE I BEAT YOU WITH YOUR PURSE."

INSPECTOR
MARGARET THATCHER

IT IS NO COINCIDENCE THAT INSPECTOR Meg (short for Margaret) Thatcher shares the same name as the former British Prime Minister. For just as the 'Iron Lady' could wield a mean handbag, so the Inspector (dubbed the 'Dragon Lady' by Ray Vecchio) is most certainly not a woman to be trifled with.

Initially described as "prickly" (which does a major disservice to porcupines), Inspector Thatcher arrives at the Canadian Consulate very much as the new broom determined to sweep everything clean. But seemingly blocking the line on this fast track to efficiency is Fraser.

Thatcher takes an instant dislike to him and consigns him to the most menial tasks. In return, the ever-polite Fraser insists on calling her "sir".

The prospect then of being stuck on a train with each other in 'All The Queen's Horses' is about as appealing as major root canal surgery, but when the train

is hijacked by terrorists, the ice maiden melts and finally expresses her true feelings for him. She is, after all, a tangled web of suppressed

Above: Thatcher initially lived up to the 'iron lady' image of her namesake. **Opposite page:** But the ice maiden melted in the company of Fraser.

emotion. But once the crisis is over, the whole incident becomes a mistake which must never be repeated, unless, as she makes very clear to Fraser, "the exact same circumstances were to repeat themselves."

As a child, Toronto-born Camilla Scott longed to be a dancer, but wound up as a pudgy teenager working on a supermarket checkout. After shedding the extra pounds, she moved to Los Angeles where she played Cherise in *Three Men and a Baby*, before appearing as Melissa Anderson in the soap *Days of Our Lives* for two years.

Next, Scott realised her childhood dream by winning the role of Polly in the Gershwin tribute musical *Crazy For You*. To get the part, she embarked on a rigorous course of seventeen dance classes a week for three months.

At the age of thirty-five, Scott's success has been sealed with her own talk show broadcast across Canada. ▼

"THANK YOU. WE CLEAN OUR OWN PERSONNEL HERE."

VICTORIA METCALF

VICTORIA METCALF FIRST CAME into Fraser's life as the driver of a getaway car during a botched Alaskan bank robbery. Bent on bringing her to justice, Fraser relentlessly pursued her across the Yukon. Trapped by a blizzard, they saved each others' lives. He kept talking to her so she wouldn't slip away, and when Fraser began to lose consciousness, she recited a poem over and over again. He became haunted by her voice. Yet when it came to the crunch, he felt obliged to turn her in. As a Mountie, it was his duty.

For eight long years she languished in jail, puzzling how, after all they had been through, Fraser could have done such a thing to her. Once released, she plotted her revenge, which ended with Fraser being arrested on suspicion of murdering her partner, Jolly. But deep down she still loved Fraser and genuinely wanted him to run away with her. But when Fraser took a bullet in the

Above: Melina Kanakaredes as Victoria Metcalf — dressed... or rather, undressed to kill. Fraser never had a chance.

back at the railway station, any potential travel plans fell by the trackside.

One of three daughters from a traditional Greek family, Melina Kanakaredes grew up in Akron, Ohio. After being runner-up in a Miss Ohio pageant, she spent fours years as Eleni Cooper in the daytime soap *The Guiding Light*, for which she won two Emmy nominations. In addition to films such as *The Long Kiss Goodnight* and *Bleeding Hearts*, she played reporter Benita Alden on *NYPD Blue*. Two days before her début on *Due South*, Melina finished shooting the Pilot for *New York News*, starring Mary Tyler Moore.

Researching her role in the ABC series *Leaving LA*, set in a coroner's office, she spent a few days as a coroner's trainee and was fortunate (or rather unfortunate) enough to attend the post-mortem examination of a particularly gruesome double homicide/suicide. ▼

"YOU WERE NEVER ONE FOR OVERSTATEMENT."

FRANCESCA VECCHIO

RAY'S SISTER FRANCESCA HAS ONE thing in common with Fraser — they always get their man. Unfortunately for Fraser, the man she has set her heart on is him. Wearing skirts that are little more than belts, she throws herself at the poor Mountie at every turn, overpowering him with sexuality and cheap perfume. Subtle she isn't.

On one occasion she leaves him shell-shocked by dropping her overcoat to reveal that she is just wearing sexy lingerie underneath. Even when she is selling sandwiches in 'We Are the Eggmen', she favours Fraser with "a good-looking, eligible bachelor discount". She certainly leaves no room for misinterpretation. And what Francesca wants, Francesca gets. So when she decides she wants sex with Fraser, she becomes a more dangerous adversary than any of Chicago's gangsters. Sadly for her, it appears that Fraser is too much of a gentleman to take advantage of her. But she won't give up without a fight.

In season three, Francesca manages to get closer still to Fraser when she takes over as Civilian Aide at the station from the recently graduated Elaine. Although at first she has some trouble mastering both the parlance of police work and the operation of a computer, Francesca inevitably brings her own personal flair to the job and soon becomes a valued member of the team. And, of course, where Francesca's concerned, personal flair extends to some very novel variations on the standard police uniform.

Canadian actress Ramona Milano describes Francesca as a "free spirit". Born in Nobleton, Ontario, Milano graduated from the Etobicoke School of Arts in 1987. Since then she has appeared in the CBS series *Top Cops*, a CBS mini series *The Last Don*, and has played a television producer in the TV movie *The Absolute Truth*. Her role as the hot-blooded Francesca earned her a Gemini award nomination for Best Supporting Actress in 1997. She has been married for three years to a teacher whom she met on a blind date, to which she freely admits she had to be dragged "kicking and screaming". Francesca's done her fair share of kicking and screaming too. ▼

Above: Ray's man-hungry sister Francesca only has eyes for Fraser. Well, most days. A scene from 'Seeing is Believing'.

"YOU SEE? NOW I HAVE THEM EXACTLY WHERE I WANT THEM. THEY THINK I'M NUTS."

ALL THE QUEEN's *horses*

IN VIEW OF HIS PEDIGREE AS A WRITER, IT was inevitable that Paul Gross would eventually turn his hand to scripting episodes of *Due South*. His first offering — 'All The Queen's Horses' — does not disappoint.

Set on a train carrying the RCMP's famous Musical Ride equestrian team on a tour of North America (accompanied by Fraser and Inspector Thatcher), the story reunites two old favourites — Fraser Sr. and 'Buck' Frobisher. The team are being filmed on board the train but show a distinct lack of animation until Fraser leads them into song. In true *Monty Python* style, the thirty-four Mounties burst into a suitably rousing chorus of 'Ride Forever' (composed by Gross and David Keeley) before suddenly being knocked unconscious mid-sentence. Buck sings on as a soloist for a few bars before he even realises something is amiss. Nothing much gets past him...

The Mounties have been gassed by terrorists posing as the film crew. Fraser climbs beneath the train where he proceeds to conduct a conversation with Buck through the lavatory bowl. Frobisher is obliged to spend much of his time there overcoming his

own gaseous problems caused by a dish of moose hock rolled in wild boar tongue and covered in gorgonzola

Above: The RCMP's Musical Ride team appear over the horizon.
Below: Father and son join forces. It's enough to stir the blood.

cheese. "Seems to follow you around for a while," he laments.

"The talk through the toilet was improvised in a New York bar," explains Gross. "Leslie and I share the

same agent and I wanted him to be a guest star, but they wouldn't tell me where he was. By chance, I ran into him in the street and told him my thoughts about him appearing in an episode which had all these Mounties trapped on a train by terrorists. And, of course, he and I were only able to talk via the john! Leslie just leapt in the air and said, 'Son, I'll do it.' Then we just let our imaginations run riot. I wrote the toilet jokes in for him. I even wrote his farts in..."

Fraser and Thatcher are soon handcuffed together, seemingly in much closer proximity than either would like. He spots a bobby pin in her hair and releases it with his teeth. The intention is to pick the lock, but at the crucial moment the pin slips down the front of her blouse. Realising this is no time to stand on ceremony, she gives him permission to retrieve it. As he nuzzles down into her bosom, the expression on her face suggests that she thinks he's taking rather too long.

Freed from his shackles, Fraser confronts one of the gang on top of the train. In the fight that follows, Fraser is thrown from the train. Thinking Fraser has fallen to his death

in the deep gorge below, Thatcher at last begins to acknowledge her true feelings for him. When he reappears, those feelings are given voice and they lock in a passionate embrace on the roof of the moving train, blissfully unaware of an approaching bridge. When they emerge from the other side, still locked in the same embrace, we see that the top of Fraser's hat has been sliced off.

As the train heads for a collision with a load of radioactive uranium, the comatose Mounties revive in unison and, in a sublime moment, carry on singing 'Ride Forever' from the exact moment in the chorus where they left off. As the terrorists make a run for it across the fields, the entire Musical Ride team appear on horseback. Bolt, the terrorist leader, remarks sardonically: "They always look so happy."

"IF WE SURVIVE THIS, REMIND ME TO MAKE SOME CHANGES TO OFFICIAL TRAVEL POLICY."

For Paul Gross, 'All The Queen's Horses' remains one of his favourite episodes. "It was just a gas to do," he says, pun presumably intentional. "It was sort of like going to camp. Leslie's very serious about what he does, but he's also a complete goofball. It was great fun watching Gordon [Pinsent] and Leslie with each other. When they weren't shooting, they'd be sitting in a compartment of the train in their red coats and howling with laughter over some bizarre joke one of them had just told the other."

Gross continues: "We more or less lived on that train. We'd pile into it in the morning and ride around the countryside for the whole day. It was a difficult episode to film and was very, very expensive, but it was a kick when we got all the horses out to shoot one of the last scenes. It's really impressive to see all those guys in red coats riding over a hill."

There was, however, one disappointment for Gross: "We were hoping to feature the real Musical Ride team. We'd told them they could choose a location which would be good for the horses and so on, but fairly late in the game they decided they weren't going to be able to do it.

"In the end I suppose it worked out for the best," concludes Gross, "because we ran into terrible complications. The first day we were shooting we started to film the end-

Above: 'Buck' Frobisher and Fraser discuss the merits, or otherwise, of moose hock rolled in wild boar tongue.

"I'M TALKING WITH A LUNATIC."

ing. There was a crystal-clear sky and it was warm the whole day. That night a storm blew in, dropped two feet of snow on the ground and took the temperature down twenty degrees. We hadn't finished the scene. We had no idea what we were going to do and prayed that it would warm up by the end of the week. It did, and we were able to finish the scene just fine, but I think something like that would probably have been a bit too complicated for people to cope with who aren't used to filming a TV series." ▼

This page: Perfect harmony? As far as Thatcher is concerned, her passionate interlude with Fraser was strictly a one-off.

FLY THE
flag

glad TIDINGS

DESPITE TROUBLED WATERS, SEASON THREE SETS SAIL...

IF *DUE SOUTH* WAS A CAT, its name would be 'Lucky', and it would only have seven lives left. For, in the harsh world of television, the chances of a show being cancelled twice and still surviving are about as likely as finding gravy stains on Fraser's uniform.

After bringing back the programme as a mid-season replacement in December 1995 and running that second series through until the following May, CBS once again cancelled. This time it seemed there would be no reprieve. So convinced were Alliance of the show's demise that they scrapped many of the sets. As far as they were concerned, *Due South* was no more. Fraser was an ex-Mountie.

But though *Due South* had seemingly failed to find its niche in America, it was a hit in many other countries (and had won another clutch of awards), and when word of the cancellation reached the BBC, Pro Sieben Media AG in Germany and TF1 in France, they offered to help Alliance and CTV bankroll a further twenty-six episodes.

"When CBS cancelled us in the States, I thought it was all over," admits Paul Gross. "Then I got a call to say that foreign broadcasters wanted to keep it

going." At first he wasn't sure, but Alliance Communications Chairman and CEO Robert Lantos convinced him that he

> ## *"Polite cop, bad cop. It might work."*

Above: Fraser adopts a novel vantage point in 'Asylum'.

had a Fraser-like duty to continue with the show. "That was one of Robert's big arguments with me about doing it again," adds Gross. "We've built this base of an audience that is so stubbornly loyal to the show, we owe it to them to finish it off with one more season."

To come up with the valued American market, the new series was launched in first-run syndication by PolyGram Television who sold it to 108 stations, representing around eighty per cent of America.

In addition to starring in the third series of *Due South*, Gross has also taken on the role of executive producer. But he has lost his old sparring partner David Marciano, who, because of other commitments, will only feature in one or two episodes. His place is taken by Canadian actor Callum Keith Rennie as Fraser's new partner, Detective Stanley Kowalski. Another newcomer to the series is Tom Melissis as Detective Thomas E. Dewey. Detective Dewey teams up with Jack Huey in the wake of Louis Gardino's death, thereby perpetuating the joke relating to Donald Duck's nephews.

"You can't replace David, but Callum is completely insane," enthuses Paul Gross about his new co-star. "Suffice to say that somebody went into his brain at

an early age and rewired everything. As a result, he brings an unpredictability to the show that has provided us an enormous amount of excitement. This gives the new series a different energy. The basic dynamic of the show and relationship remain the same, but the humour is a little different."

Looking back on the CBS involvement, Jeff King says: "I think CBS never really knew exactly what we were — cop show, action show, comedy. Truth is, I think we were all three. We didn't always hit the right notes, but when we did, the three genres met in a truly wonderful and unique result.

"None of us wanted to do a straight cop show," he continues, "because we had a guy in a red suit with brass buttons who held doors open and said thank you. An odd, funny cop. But we also had a tough Chicago cop and the show was set in his world. So it had to operate by some of the rules of a cop show. I know David Marciano would have preferred more such rules, but the series was more than just a cop show. I think we were breaking new ground." ▼

Above: Fraser, Welsh and Thatcher search the Great Lakes for lost treasure in 'Mountie on the Bounty'.
Below: Callum Keith Rennie as Detective Stanley Kowalski.

BURNING DOWN THE *house*

'**B**URNING DOWN THE HOUSE', THE opening episode to season three, was born out of necessity. Paul Gross reveals: "Because the set for Fraser's apartment had been thrown out when we thought the series was cancelled, we had to explain it away by saying his apartment had burned down. Then we torched Ray Vecchio's house too. That was just for fun," laughs Gross. "We were in a burning mood by then." The police station set had also been dismantled but was subsequently rebuilt.

The story begins with Fraser returning to Chicago from a working vacation in the far north during which, in his own inimitable way, he managed to destroy $733,000 (Canadian) worth of public and private property in pursuit of a litterbug. His homecoming is not exactly a happy one, arriving as he does just as his apart-ment goes up in flames. What's more, there's no sign of Ray and everyone seems cagey as to his whereabouts. To add to Fraser's confusion, a new detective appears at Ray's desk and passes himself off as Ray Vecchio, complete with Green 1971 Buick Riviera. All except Fraser seem per-fectly happy with the explanation.

Even the handing out of gifts from his vacation fails to elicit a satisfactory answer. Detective Huey's is a par-ticularly inappropriate genuine beluga whale-bone sextant, perfect for triangulating one's location in a vast,

Above: Greta Garbo (really!) carries on the work of performance arsonist Zoltan Motherwell by rigging the Riv to burst into flames.

open territory with no distinguishing landmarks. "Yeah, I can see how this can come in real handy in Chicago, Fraser," says Huey, a mite caustically.

Before Fraser can solve the riddle of the two Rays, he receives an anony-mous tip that the Vecchio home is the next target of a performance arsonist. Fraser and the new Ray speed to the burning house where the Mountie risks his life to rescue Francesca, Tony and the goldfish.

Perfume bottle fragments discovered in the rubble at the scenes of both fires lead to one Zoltan Motherwell, currently languishing in a hos-pital for the criminally insane, and bearing a bitter grudge against Fraser and Vecchio for cutting his career short. Motherwell's girlfriend, now calling herself Greta Garbo, has been carrying on his good work.

Trying to guess Greta's next target, it eventually dawns on Fraser and 'Ray' that they are sitting in it. The Riv has been rigged to go up in flames during the high-speed pursuit of Ms

"MY HOUSE IS BURNING DOWN AND YOU'RE WORRIED ABOUT A STOP SIGN?"

 Above: Fraser surveys the burnt-out wreck of his apartment. Still, a new coat of paint can work wonders.

Garbo. In a bid to locate the device, Fraser climbs on to the roof of the speeding car while 'Ray', driving, decides to reveal all about his mystery identity before he is blown to pieces. Unfortunately, Fraser can't hear a word. As smoke turns to flame, they steer the blazing car through the city streets, eventually extinguishing the fire by driving straight into Lake Michigan.

Back at the station, Fraser at last uncovers the truth about his new partner. He is Detective Stanley Kowalski, but he is masquerading as Ray in order to provide cover for Vecchio who has infiltrated the mob and can't be reached.

"It was a challenge having to start almost from scratch with a new co-star," says Paul Gross. "We had a number of storylines we were working on that had David Marciano in mind. With his departure, we had to undertake a considerable rewrite. The basic idea of 'Burning Down the House' was to introduce Callum in the context of a plot which was moving so quickly that Fraser wouldn't have time to really question Kowalski's assertion that he was Vecchio and that seemed to indicate someone was hunting them."

Playing Motherwell is *Due South* director and creative producer George Bloomfield. "Paul Gross asked me to play it," says Bloomfield, "and I was very flattered and said yes. Then I had to do it... and was terrified."

For David Marciano, his brief appearance as the old Ray Vecchio in 'Burning Down the House' was an emotional experience he will never forget. "The anticipation was nerve-racking," he admits. "The moment I

Above: Litterers beware. Fraser lets no criminal act, no matter how innocuous, go unpunished.

"AH, CONSTABLE. YOU RETURN. UPON REFLECTION I IMAGINE THAT PLEASES ME."

walked on the set was like the birthing of a new star and the performing of the scene was beyond exhilarating. After I was done, I looked around at the faces I had become friends with over the past two seasons. They had already been shooting the third season with the new Ray for two months, so my return to the set was tension-filled.

"Callum was also filming that day and no one knew how we would react to each other. He is a very nice man. We had a good talk, after I had finished filming, about the new Ray and what my thoughts were on the approach of the new character toward the show in general."

In conclusion, Marciano sums up his feelings for Ray and the series: "As I look back on that day and my experience, I realise how much I love Ray Vecchio and how much I loved making *Due South*." ▼

This page: Kowalski (alias Ray) and Fraser rescue Francesca from the burning family home.

DETECTIVE STANLEY KOWALSKI

NAMED AFTER THE CHIEF PROTAgonist in *A Streetcar Named Desire* (his father was a Brando fan), Stanley Raymond Kowalski is a tough-talking American who consistently belies his oft-voiced vow that he won't risk his neck for anyone. His record includes three citations for bravery.

Never having liked his full name, Kowalski prefers to be called Ray. A happy coincidence, given the nature of his current assignment as stand-in for Ray Vecchio.

As an undercover cop, Kowalski understands that loneliness comes with the territory, but in this case he soon discovers unexpected and pleasant bonuses in the shape of Fraser, his 'sister' Francesca and her large Italian family.

Broody, secretive, invariably scruffy and no respecter of authority, Kowalski tends not to share Fraser's ideology. To him, it's just a job. He's also shortsighted and, whilst a crack shot with his glasses on, without them he is a danger to low-flying aircraft.

He was a keen boxer until retiring from the ring when he married Stella. The pair are now divorced (Ray wanted children, Stella wasn't ready to give up her career) and she is the Assistant State's Attorney. But the passion is still there and he hopes to win her back some day.

Ever since 1974 Kowalski has been haunted by bank robber Marcus Ellery, who terrified and humiliated him during a robbery he witnessed as a teenager. That incident ultimately led to him becoming a cop, though not necessarily for all the right reasons.

Surprisingly, one of Kowalski's favourite forms of relaxation — a passion he and Stella shared since they were childhood sweethearts — is ballroom dancing.

Callum Keith Rennie was born in Sunderland, England, and raised in Alberta. He was a stage actor in Edmonton, where, working on the university's campus radio station, he first caught the acting bug. Moving to Vancouver, Rennie appeared in a number of series produced locally, including *Lonesome Dove*, *Highlander* and *The X-Files*. In 1993, he won a Genie Award nomination as Best Supporting Actor for his role as the nerdish boyfriend in the movie *Double Happiness*. Rennie has gone on to play a recovering junkie in *Curtis's Charm*, laconic guitarist Johnny Talent in Bruce McDonald's punk rockumentary *Hard Core Logo* and con man Jerry Bines in CBC's *For Those Who Hunt The Wounded Down*, a performance which led to critics comparing thirty-seven-year-old Rennie to James Dean.

As one scribe sums up: "He has the rugged cool of a bad boy who has been to hell and back, looks better for it, and now humours the camera with good behaviour." ▼

Above: Kowalski's meeting with gang boss Andreas Volpe in 'Asylum' leaves him framed for Volpe's murder.

"WHICH RAY VECCHIO? THE DETECTIVE FORMERLY KNOWN AS RAY VECCHIO OR THE CURRENT DETECTIVE KNOWN AS THE FORMER RAY VECCHIO?"

Above: Callum Keith Rennie
as the enigmatic Kowalski.
Left: Kowalski plays chess
with Albert Hanrahan
in 'Spy vs. Spy'.

HEADS
you win

CALLUM KEITH
RENNIE ARGUES
THE TOSS

IT'S FAIR TO SAY THAT BY any standards Callum Keith Rennie's audition for *Due South* was unconventional. "Paul Gross asked me whether I thought I could play Kowalski," recalls Rennie. "We were in a bar and we tossed a coin. I called right, but even then we had to do the best of three..."

But then Rennie has always thrived on being different from the crowd. As a kid, he listened to Canadian punk bands and sported a Mohawk haircut and admits that he spent most of his twenties drinking. At thirty-three, he finally quit. "I got a piece of glass in my eye in a bar fight. I thought: 'This has gone far enough'."

Not a man for using a dozen words when one will do, he admits that television people sometimes find him "difficult", but maintains that this is due to his refreshingly honest attitude towards the acting profession.

He is very choosy about his roles and turned down the recurring part of 'Ratboy' (Agent Alex Krycek) in *The X-Files* for fear of being tied down to something for too long. So his one-year contract on *Due South* suits him fine.

"I'd only seen a couple of episodes of *Due South* before landing the part and I'd never worked with Paul Gross before," says Rennie. "Although a lot of my previous roles have been bad guys, I didn't feel the need to do any research with the police. Anyway, I play a cop like I play a bad guy.

"Kowalski's the sort of guy who acts before he thinks. Although he appears hard on the outside, he's really quite soft. It's pretty much a learning competition between him and Fraser, with each fulfilling a quality lacking in the other."

Paul Gross concurs: "At its core, their relationship is about trusting each other implicitly, but on the surface there is the friction that arises between two people whose backgrounds are poles apart. It's a different relationship from the one Fraser had with Ray. It's still city cop/Mountie, but Kowalski's just kind of crazy." Gross adds: "As for Callum, he's a very sexy guy on screen, an intriguing presence."

Ask Rennie what it was like being the new guy joining an established series, and his reply is: "Complicated yet simple!" He is more forthcoming when discussing scenes from 'Mountie on the Bounty', the two-part finale to season three, wherein Fraser and Kowalski are saved from drowning by being blown sky high — literally.

Rennie explains the problems he encountered: "It was definitely my most uncomfortable experience on *Due South* to date. I was slung up in a harness 100ft up in the air, hanging from a crane, to simulate flying after being soaked in cold water. I had bruises on my back for two weeks." ▼

> *"This is Chicago, Fraser. The only time people use chainsaws is when they're trying to get rid of a body."*

This page: Kowalski and Fraser in
'Spy vs. Spy' (above) and 'Mountie on
the Bounty' (left).

Above: 'Chinatown'.

THE PILOT
WRITER: Paul Haggis
DIRECTOR: Fred Gerber
The hunt for his father's killer takes Constable Benton Fraser to Chicago, where he teams up with Detective Ray Vecchio. With the help of a little mud-tasting and a nose ID, the trail leads to Fraser Sr.'s ex-partner, Gerrard. The climax is a high-speed dog-sled ride through the snow-covered Canadian wilderness. (see pages 14–17)

season ONE

1 FREE WILLIE
WRITERS: Kathy Slevin & Paul Haggis
DIRECTOR: George Bloomfield
Fraser sets out to prove the innocence of a twelve-year-old purse snatcher accused of armed robbery. Although the boy, Willie Lambert, is a habitual thief and compulsive liar, Fraser persuades Ray that the boy is good at heart and will keep his promise of being able to lead them to the real culprits. But first there is a dash through the park by horse and carriage.

2 DIEFENBAKER'S DAY OFF
WRITER: Kathy Slevin
DIRECTOR: Joe Scanlan
A six-year-old girl appeals to Fraser to help her Daddy who appears to be somewhat accident prone. Fraser soon discovers why — her father, Charlie, is the 'Fall Guy' for a personal injury fraud ring. For $200 a time, he throws himself in front of moving vehicles. Meanwhile Diefenbaker goes sightseeing alone in Chicago and attracts the interest of the local dog catcher.

3 MANHUNT
WRITER: Paul Haggis
DIRECTOR: Paul Lynch
When Sergeant Duncan 'Buck' Frobisher, legendary Mountie and best friend of Fraser's late father, goes missing a week before retirement, his daughter Julie asks Fraser for help. (see pages 34–35)

4 THEY EAT HORSES, DON'T THEY?
WRITER: Stephen Neigher
DIRECTOR: Tim Bond
On his first trip to a supermarket, Fraser senses that the 'All Beef' label on a pound of ground meat may be a shade optimistic. As he and Ray pursue a gang who have been selling wild horses for slaughter, they find themselves held captive in a refrigerated meat locker, where Fraser suggests they wrap themselves in animal carcasses to retain body heat and survive.

5 PIZZAS AND PROMISES
WRITER: David Shore
DIRECTOR: George Bloomfield
Ray and Fraser go undercover as used car salesmen to solve the mystery of a stolen car ring. In the course of their investigation, they must contend with a sleazy salesman, his libidinous wife, Fraser's futile attempts at lying and Ray being trapped in the trunk of a car on the fast lane to the bottom of Lake Michigan.

6 CHINATOWN
WRITER: David Cole
DIRECTOR: Lyndon Chubbuck
While dining out in Chinatown, Fraser overhears a kidnapping. The victim, the son of restaurateur Henry Lee, has been seized in an effort to dissuade his father from standing up to local gang lord Charlie Wong. Lee sees no option but to bow to Wong's demands, but Fraser urges him to 'trust in the law'. However, two power-hungry FBI agents threaten the entire operation and put the boy's life in jeopardy.

7 CHICAGO HOLIDAY (PART 1)
WRITERS: Jeff King & Paul Haggis
DIRECTOR: Paul Lynch
A seemingly innocuous Consulate assignment escalates into a wild ride for Fraser when his teenage charge, diplomat's daughter Christina Nichols, chooses that night to rebel against her repressive lifestyle. Alas, Fraser isn't the only one trying to keep pace with Christina. For she has acquired a matchbook which a ruthless killer is desperate to get his hands on.

8 CHICAGO HOLIDAY (PART 2)

WRITERS: Jeff King & Paul Haggis
DIRECTOR: Lyndon Chubbuck

Wild child Christina Nichols has managed to shake off Fraser but remains the target for the killer hunted by Ray and the rest of the Chicago police force. Fraser's attempts to save her life take him to a tacky bar and see him tobogganing down an escalator and plummeting down a garbage chute.

9 A COP, A MOUNTIE AND A BABY

WRITER: Kathy Slevin (story by Peter Colley & Kathy Slevin)
DIRECTOR: Steve DiMarco

Discovering a baby in the back seat of the Riv, the resourceful Fraser tracks down the father via a series of clues drawn from the baby's food and clothing. After Ray's Armani coat has been covered in vomit, he and Fraser learn that the mother abandoned the infant to stop her husband selling it to pay off his debts. While Fraser attempts to convince the father of the greater value of the love of a child, Diefenbaker adopts a more proactive approach and won't let the baby out of his sight.

10 THE GIFT OF THE WHEELMAN

WRITER: Paul Haggis
DIRECTOR: Gerry Ciccoritti

When a gang of gun-toting Santas hold up a Chicago bank, Fraser's and Ray's investigations lead them to the getaway driver, who only went on the raid to provide for his son and who now plans to doublecross his partners in crime. While Fraser must make the wheelman understand that the most valuable gift a father can give to his son is an example of how to be a man, Detectives Huey and Gardino are rounding up every department store Santa in town, only to end up with a station full of Elvis impersonators!

11 YOU MUST REMEMBER THIS

WRITER: Peter Lefcourt
DIRECTOR: David Warry-Smith

A kiss is just a kiss, except Ray is sure it means more as he pursues the woman of his dreams, the beautiful and mysterious Suzanne Chapin, after she rescues him from a hit-and-run driver. The trail leads him to a gang of arms dealers and a showdown between the gang's forty ton army truck and Ray's beloved 1971 Buick Riviera.

12 HAWK AND A HANDSAW

WRITERS: David Shore & Paul Haggis (story by David Shore)
DIRECTOR: George Bloomfield

Accompanying Ray to a clinic for his annual psychological examination, Fraser saves the life of a patient who is desperately searching for someone named Ty. Sensing something amiss, Fraser has himself admitted, simply by telling the authorities that he is a Mountie in Chicago with a lip-reading wolf. Once inside, he hears frightening stories of a sinister blue room where patients are taken to die.

13 AN EYE FOR AN EYE

WRITERS: Carla Kettner, Kathy Slevin & Jeff King (story by Carla Kettner)
DIRECTOR: Steve DiMarco

Fraser inspires a group of senior citizens to take a stand against crime and form a neighbourhood watch. Unfortunately, one septuagenarian turns vigilante and exacts his own brand of justice — with a baseball bat. At the seniors' centre, Dief is befriended by Gladys, a compulsive knitter. It seems only a matter of time before he is obliged to wear crocheted booties on all four paws.

Above: 'Hawk and a Handsaw'.

14 THE MAN WHO KNEW TOO LITTLE

WRITER: Frank Siracusa
DIRECTOR: George Bloomfield

Assigned the task of escorting pathological liar Ian MacDonald back to Canada to face — unsurprisingly — perjury charges, Fraser and Ray meet three Canadians *en route*. Like all Canadians, they're polite, well groomed and respectful. But unlike most Canadians, they're also killers whose mission is to prevent MacDonald from ever being able to tell the truth. Our heroes can only save his life at the expense of the Riv.

Above: 'A Cop, a Mountie and a Baby'.

Above: 'The Blue Line'.

Having covered for Fraser as the Consulate doorman, Ray arrives at the dump in the nick of time and convinces the fiancé that it is all just a misunderstanding. But the latter's conciliatory mood is shattered by the news that his betrothed may be in love with someone else... a man in a red uniform.

19 HEAVEN AND EARTH
WRITERS: Phil Bedard & Larry Lalonde
DIRECTOR: David Warry-Smith
With Ray anguishing over whether his sister and Fraser slept together, a psychic down-and-out with chilli on his fingers provides the only link to a kidnapped girl. The man, Garret, claims to have had visions about the kidnapping. Only Fraser believes Garret and trusts him to take them to the girl before it's too late.

15 THE WILD BUNCH
WRITERS: Kathy Slevin & Jeff King
DIRECTOR: Richard Lewis
When Dief is arrested for biting an animal control officer, Fraser isn't sure whether the wolf's uncharacteristic behaviour is caused by love or a return to his wild ways. (see pages 38–39)

16 THE BLUE LINE
WRITER: David Shore
DIRECTOR: George Bloomfield
Fraser's illusions are shattered when he meets up with childhood friend and hockey star Mark Smithbauer in the middle of a liquor store shoot-out. For Smithbauer is in deep with a bookie who paid him to throw a game. The bookie seeks vengeance in a manic cars versus skates chase through the icy streets of Chicago.

17 THE DEAL
WRITER: Peter Lefcourt
DIRECTOR: George Mendeluk
A humble shoemaker incurs the wrath of Mafia mobster Frank Zuko, Ray's boyhood rival. When Fraser is beaten up trying to protect the shoemaker, Ray sets up a one-on-one confrontation with Zuko in a bid to halt his reign of terror. Meanwhile, Fraser is living in fear of Ray's sister Francesca who has decided it's about time she and the dashing Mountie had sex. Will she get her man?

18 AN INVITATION TO ROMANCE
WRITERS: Deborah Rennard & Paul Haggis
DIRECTOR: George Bloomfield
Caught in a compromising situation with a bride-to-be (he's found hiding under her wedding dress while she is wearing it), Fraser falls foul of the prospective groom who opts to dispose of the pair of them at the city dump.

20 AND 21 VICTORIA'S SECRET
WRITERS: Paul Haggis & David Shore
DIRECTOR: Paul Haggis
Bank robber Victoria Metcalf, the only woman Fraser ever loved, suddenly appears in Chicago. (see pages 44–49)

22 LETTING GO
WRITERS: Jeff King & Kathy Slevin
DIRECTOR: George Bloomfield

Above: 'The Deal'.

Nursing a gunshot wound in hospital, Fraser also bears the emotional scars caused by Victoria's betrayal. But he and his beautiful young physical therapist, Jill Kennedy, soon find themselves taking more than a passing interest in the blackmail plot taking place across the hall from his room. Just as Ray fears that his friendship with Fraser is over, he throws himself in front of a bullet meant for the Mountie. And before you know it, the pair are best buddies again.

season **TWO**
----

23 NORTH
WRITER: Jeff King
DIRECTOR: Richard J. Lewis
A vacation up north hits a snag when Fraser and Ray's plane is hijacked by an escaped killer who literally bales out on them. In the ensuing crash, Fraser is left concussed and blinded, so it is largely down to Ray to steer his friend back to civilisation and away from the clutches of the killer who is stalking them through the woods. To complicate matters further, both dead fathers are on hand to offer their own brand of advice.

Above: 'The Witness'.

Above: 'Mask'.

24 VAULT
WRITER: Kathy Slevin (story by Jeff King, Paul Haggis & Kathy Slevin)
DIRECTOR: Steve DiMarco
Declared dead by a computer error, Ray heads to the bank to sort things out, only for he and Fraser to stumble across a robbery. To protect the bank's money, Fraser instinctively locks himself and his partner in the vault and, to take the robbers by surprise, sets off the sprinkler system. Soon he and Ray are nose deep in rising water. And outside Francesca is being held hostage.

25 THE WITNESS
WRITER: Peter Mohan
DIRECTOR: George Bloomfield
When Ray is thrown in jail for contempt of court after his star witness perjures herself, Fraser decides the case needs investigating from the inside. So he gets himself arrested for stealing a box of Milk Duds and befriends the inmates as their library monitor.

26 BIRD IN THE HAND
WRITER: Paul Haggis
DIRECTOR: Paul Haggis
Gerrard, the man who killed Fraser's father, is on the loose in Chicago and the FBI want Fraser to bring him in alive. (see pages 54–55)

27 THE PROMISE
WRITER: Michael Teversham
DIRECTOR: George Bloomfield
A high-class call girl is murdered for an electronic organiser which contains the

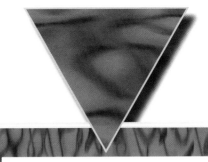

MASK

MOST OF THE STORIES ON *DUE SOUTH* are pure fiction, but a few are inspired by real events. One such example is 'Mask' from season two. Writer Jeff King explains: "Two writers — Nancy Merritt Bell and Michael McKinley — had pitched us an idea about Fraser in the world of art. That was an area which interested me so I was looking for a *Due South* kind of way of looking at that world. I got the idea for 'Mask' after reading an account of how a very rare aboriginal transformation mask — which comprised two pieces that are attached — had been separated and the two parts each sold to a different museum by European missionaries. The mask was significant to the culture and religion of the West Coast peoples who originally made it, so I imagined a story about someone retrieving it. If I hadn't read that account, I might never have known about the masks nor done the story."

names of her illustrious clients, many of whom she had been blackmailing. It falls into the hands of a young pickpocket and it is up to Fraser and Ray to prevent her and her brother from becoming the killer's next victims. Meanwhile, Fraser has to contend with his new boss, the prickly Inspector Meg Thatcher, who is moaning about the theft of her brooch.

28 MASK
WRITER: Jeff King (story by Nancy Merritt Bell, Michael McKinley & Jeff King)
DIRECTOR: David Warry-Smith
The theft of two valuable aboriginal masks from a museum earns Fraser a visit from old friend Eric, a native leader

Above: 'Starman'.

who believes the crime may have been committed by David, a boy from his village. Eric is anxious for the objects to be returned safely to their rightful owners, the Tsimshian people, and to this end, he sets up home in Fraser's apartment, complete with a traditional sweat lodge. Ray finally asks State's Attorney Louise St. Laurent for a date.

29 JULIET IS BLEEDING
WRITERS: Kathy Slevin & Jeff King
DIRECTOR: George Bloomfield
Ray finds himself torn between his love for a mobster's sister and his quest for revenge against Mafia don Frank Zuko. (see pages 58–61)

30 ONE GOOD MAN (AKA THANK YOU KINDLY, MR. CAPRA)
WRITERS: Kathy Slevin & Jeff King (story by Frank Siracusa)
DIRECTOR: Malcolm Cross
Fraser's attempts to clean up his apartment building work well — until the new landlord decides to evict everyone. With the aid of cherry throat lozenges, Fraser brings the case before the City Council where he fights for his belief that one good man can make a difference.

31 THE EDGE
WRITER: Seth Freeman
DIRECTOR: Richard J. Lewis
Fraser and Ray are teamed with Anita Cortez, a spitfire Mexican secret service agent, to protect delegates at a NAFTA summit. But Fraser fears he is losing his edge after being repeatedly outwitted by an unknown assassin, a feeling underlined when he is relegated to writing name tags for the opening-night dinner. Serving as a waiter in a white tux, he ensures that the killer gets his just desserts.

32 WE ARE THE EGGMEN
WRITERS: Michael Teversham & Peter Mohan (story by James Kramer)
DIRECTOR: George Bloomfield
Having rescued the driver of a lorry from the edge of a precipice, Fraser is rather surprised to be landed with a $10,000,000 lawsuit relating to broken eggs. While Fraser and Thatcher infiltrate the egg factory, Ray ponders over whether to share his lottery win with Francesca.

33 STARMAN
WRITER: Frank Siracusa
DIRECTOR: David Warry-Smith
Compulsive liar Ian MacDonald asks Fraser and Ray for help in tracing Audrey, his girlfriend of forty minutes, who he claims has been abducted by aliens. The trio travel to a top-secret military installation located in Roswell, Illinois, in the hope of getting some answers.

34 SOME LIKE IT RED
WRITERS: Luciano & Elizabeth Comici
DIRECTOR: Gilbert Shilton
Ray's ex-girlfriend Anne, now a nun and head teacher at a Catholic girls' school, appeals for some assistance in locating a missing girl. (see pages 68–69)

35 WHITE MEN CAN'T JUMP TO CONCLUSIONS
WRITER: David Shore
DIRECTOR: Steve DiMarco
Collecting Fraser's Mountie boots from the repairers, he and Ray stumble across a shooting. Prime suspect is Tyree, full-time gang member and part-time basketball player, but Fraser is convinced of his innocence. Fraser's search for the truth brings him to the attention of the local gang boss, who targets our hero for elimination.

36 ALL THE QUEEN'S HORSES
WRITER: Paul Gross (story by Paul Gross, Paul Quarrington & John Krizanc)
DIRECTOR: George Bloomfield
A train carrying Fraser, Thatcher, Frobisher and the RCMP's renowned equestrian team, the Musical Ride, is taken over by a terrorist group. (see pages 74–77)

37 BODY LANGUAGE
WRITER: James Kramer
DIRECTOR: John Cassar
Fraser's gallant rescue of a stuffed bunny endears him to the furry creature's owner, exotic dancer Ida. In return, she tips him off about a forthcoming crime and, when the tip proves accurate, Fraser and Ray try to track the mysterious informant to a strip club. Once there, the trio find themselves caught in the crossfire between rival factions.

38 THE DUEL
WRITER: Seth Freeman
DIRECTOR: Gilbert Shilton
Released from prison on parole,

Charles Carver is out for revenge on the cop who busted him — Ray. When the Assistant State's Attorney is attacked by a frozen turkey as she steps into the shower, it starts a chilling sequence of riddles which grow ever more menacing for Ray, his family and his friends.

39 RED, WHITE OR BLUE

WRITER: Paul Gross (story by Paul Gross & John Krizanc)

DIRECTOR: George Bloomfield

To Ray's annoyance, Fraser is receiving all the media attention at the trial of terrorist Randal Bolt (from 'All The Queen's Horses'). But when Bolt's family help the prisoner to escape and take Fraser and Ray hostage, Ray finds himself well and truly in the limelight. The pair are strapped to a bomb set to explode if their combined heart rates exceed 200 beats per minute.

40 FLASHBACK

WRITERS: Peter Mohan & Michael Teversham

DIRECTOR: Gilbert Shilton

In pursuit of fleeing diamond thieves, Fraser is thrown from the back of the getaway van and sustains a head injury which causes amnesia. He can't remember who or what he is or the details of the van's licence plate, the only clue to the robbers. With a hostage seized by the raiders in grave danger, Ray must work hard to get his friend's memory back.

season THREE

41 BURNING DOWN THE HOUSE

WRITER: Paul Gross

DIRECTOR: George Bloomfield

Fraser returns from a working vacation in the far north to find his life in Chicago turned upside down. (see pages 82–85)

42 ECLIPSE

WRITER: John Krizanc

DIRECTOR: Richard J. Lewis

With Ray under investigation for corruption, Fraser goes in search of Kowalski, the only man who can clear up the charges. But first Fraser must assist his new partner in exorcising the spectre of bank robber Marcus Ellery.

Above: 'I Coulda Been a Defendant'.

43 I COULDA BEEN A DEFENDANT

WRITER: Jeff King

DIRECTOR: Jimmy Kaufman

By trying to thank a man who saved a boy's life, Fraser and Kowalski accidentally blow his cover as a protected Federal witness. As the situation becomes life-threatening and the good guys are hopelessly outnumbered, Elaine's entire Police Academy graduating class comes charging over the hill to save the day.

Above: 'Bounty Hunter'.

44 STRANGE BEDFELLOWS

WRITER: R. B. Carney

DIRECTOR: George Bloomfield

Under the pretence of enforcing laws against 'lascivious' acts in public, Kowalski spies on his ex-wife Stella and her influential new boyfriend, Frank Orsini. While on 'surveillance', Fraser spots an armed man in an alley. Duly impressed, Orsini requests that Fraser and Kowalski be assigned as his round-the-clock bodyguards. They must accompany him everywhere... even on his dates with Stella.

45 MOUNTIE & SOUL

WRITER: R. B. Carney

DIRECTOR: Steve DiMarco

Kowalski is coaching in a boxing programme for gang kids. When his protégé, Levon, seriously injures another kid in the ring, Fraser and Kowalski begin an investigation that leads them into the seamier side of the fight game.

46 BOUNTY HUNTER

WRITER: George Walker

DIRECTOR: Steve DiMarco

With the Chicago police force in the grip of an illegal strike action known as

Above: 'Mountie & Soul'.

the 'blue flu', Fraser and Kowalski help bounty hunter Janet Morse track down a bail jumper from Montana. Just as things heat up between Fraser and Janet, he discovers that she and the bail jumper have a few secrets of their own.

47 SEEING IS BELIEVING

WRITER: Michael Teversham
DIRECTOR: Steve DiMarco

Kowalski, Welsh and Thatcher all witness a murder at a local shopping mall but, even with two suspects in custody, they can't agree on the culprit. Fraser, who was apprehending a purse-snatcher at the time, has to resort to hypnosis to unravel the mystery.

48 SPY VS. SPY

WRITER: David Cole
DIRECTOR: Paul Lynch

Fraser's friend Albert Hanrahan gets taxi signals on the metal plate in his head and waits for the day he will be 'activated' in the service of his country. His insistence that he is a spy is given credence when he intercepts a secret message, as a result of which Fraser and Kowalski find themselves at the centre of a deadly arms transaction. In order to solve the case, Fraser pits his wits against a notorious Russian spy and takes up ballet.

49 DEAD GUY RUNNING

WRITER: Julie Lacey
DIRECTOR: George Bloomfield

Fraser and Kowalski discover a dead guy — an old adversary of Ray Vecchio's — sealed into the wall of an interrogation room. The word was he had walked on a technicality. Trouble is, it doesn't look like he walked too far. To clear Ray's name, Fraser arranges for the body to be hidden while he investigates, but a fierce gun battle at the station ends with the corpse being held hostage.

50 PERFECT STRANGERS

WRITER: David Cole
DIRECTOR: Frances Danberger

The investigation into a pair of mysteriously linked murders takes Kowalski to Toronto. Canada spooks Kowalski — the people are so polite. It's like an entire nation of Frasers. And what is it with all these languages? Meanwhile Inspector Thatcher is developing maternal yearnings and Fraser fears she may want him to be part of the 'process'.

51 ASYLUM

WRITER: Paul Quarrington
DIRECTOR: George Bloomfield

When Kowalski is framed for the murder of a gang boss, Fraser arrests him in order to provide asylum at the Canadian Consulate. While Fraser tracks down the real killer, Constable Turnbull tries to show Kowalski some real Canadian hospitality. Any hopes Kowalski has of escaping are blocked by Diefenbaker.

52 MOUNTIE ON THE BOUNTY (PART 1)

WRITERS: Paul Gross and R. B. Carney (story by John Krizanc)
DIRECTOR: George Bloomfield

Fraser and Kowalksi are thinking of dissolving their partnership, but when a mysterious sailor dies muttering 'treasure chest', they embark on a murder case which leaves them trapped below decks on a sinking Great Lakes freighter.

53 MOUNTIE ON THE BOUNTY (PART 2)

WRITERS: Paul Gross and R. B. Carney (story by John Krizanc)
DIRECTOR: George Bloomfield

Desperately seeking an escape from the

Above: 'Mountie on the Bounty'.

sinking vessel, Fraser and Kowalski spot a 'ghost ship' in the distance. It turns out to have close links to a Chicago bullion robbery in which six guards were killed. Thatcher enlists the help of an eccentric Mountie named Sergeant Sam and a replica of the HMS *Bounty* as she prepares to sail to the rescue.

US AIRDATES (CBS)

PILOT FILM: 26 April 1994.
SEASON ONE: 22 Sept 1994 –
9 June 1995
SEASON TWO: 1 Dec 1995 –
24 May 1996

UK AIRDATES (BBC)

PILOT FILM: 9 May 1995
SEASON ONE: 16 May –
28 Nov 1995
SEASON TWO: 27 July – 12 Oct 1996; 4 Jan – 1 Feb 1997

CANADIAN AIRDATES (CTV)

PILOT FILM: 15 September 1994
SEASON ONE: 22 Sept 1994 –
1 June 1995
SEASON TWO: 9 Nov 1995 –
12 Sept 1996
SEASON THREE: 14 Sept 1997 –
22 March 1998